THE HELL-RAKES

Jack Loudan

Secret societies for debauchery and depravity;
Black Mass orgies, organised by the
notorious Hell Fire Club, in which leading
politicians and public figures of the day took
part; the seduction of teenage girls by
roistering aristocrats, and a private 'harem' of
whores for the members of the London Stock
Exchange—widespread hell-rakery by men of
wealth and culture. And these libertines
brought to the art of seduction the wit of the
Age of Reason and the elegance of the
Georgians.

The Hell-Rakes

Jack Loudan

BOOKS FOR YOU

47 Highgate Hill, N.19

CONTENTS

ACKNOWLEDGEMENTS

Illustrations:

Plates 2, 4, 5, 6, 9, 10 and 11 are reproduced by permission of The Trustees of the British Museum; Plate 7 by permission of the Trustees of the National Gallery, London; Plates 1, 3, 8 and 12 by permission of the Trustees of the National Portrait Gallery, London.

INTRODUCTION

It has been said that the two most fascinating subjects in the world are sex and the eighteenth century. The story of eighteenth century British rakery is certainly fascinating; it is also shocking.

London had numerous secret clubs for depravity and debauchery; the notorious Hell Fire Club organised elaborate ritualistic orgies in which leading politicians and public figures of the day took part; roistering aristocrats vied as to the number of young girls they could seduce; brothel "Madams" produced child virgins for the dissolute gentry; the London Stock Exchange had its private "harem" of prostitutes; beautiful young courtesans were exchanged or given as presents by their noble protectors. Satirical prints and broadsheets depicted the moral disorder of the times. The politicians were, in the main, corrupt. The Georgian kings were themselves licentious. Highwaymen infested the countryside, and being robbed by footpads was the least of one's dangers in the towns and cities, where gangs of young "Mohocks" inflicted terrible injuries and humiliations on their victims, male and female, for what would now be called "kicks."

Yet, in the main, the rakes were men of great intellect, wit and culture who brought to their libertinism the stylised elegance of the Georgians. And there can be no doubt that the period has an infectious vitality (a minor facet of this appeal was the huge box-office success of the film "Tom Jones").

Jack Loudan, whose biography of Amanda McKittrick Ross is now a much sought collectors' item, has here written of the eighteenth century British rakes and rogues, courtesans and strumpets, with the combined gusto and irony that the subject requires. Not surprisingly, for much of the spicy gossip of the times he draws on the letters of Horace Walpole, whose avowed aim was "collecting the follies of the age for the information of posterity." Like him, Jack Loudan might say : "for myself I love anything that marks a character strongly."

JAMES HEWITT

THE YEARS OF SWEETNESS

Those who did not live before 1789 knew not the sweetness of life.

Charles Maurice Talleyrand, priest and politician, was possibly right when he made that remark about his native France. John Wilmot, Earl of Rochester, could have said much the same thing about the England he knew. He summed up his philosophy in these few words :

The three Businesses of this Age are Women, Drinking and Politicks.

Rochester was the most likeable English rake of all time. Not even Casanova could have excelled him in the pursuit of lovely women. He roamed the streets of London like the Caliph of Baghdad in search of new experiences. He wrote reams of verse about the delights of making love. In a highly bibulous age, he could drink most of his friends under the table.

For the rich people like himself life in this sceptred isle was a continuous merry-go-round of pleasure and sensual enjoyment. The poor could not afford so much self indulgence but they were reasonably happy. The rich ate well, drank well and lived graciously. They had no inhibitions about sex.

The Englishman was always as interested in seduction as his Latin counterparts. Shakespeare could have taught any of his Continental contemporaries a thing or two about women. So could the dramatists who followed him. Censorship as we know it now did not exist.

"Our theatre is in such a state of indecency," wrote Jeremy Collier, "that any virtuous lady who wishes to go there must wear a mask." But were the ladies so virtuous who went to see plays like John Ford's comedy, *'Tis a Pity She's a Whore?* The truth is that Englishwomen in those days were as lascivious as the men. It was not a matter of birth or breeding.

"Pretty, witty Nell Gwynn" endeared herself to the hearts of her countrywomen for her forthrightness and sense of humour—even more so because she was no respecter of persons or rank. Charles II, when he saw her act on one occasion complimented her on the perfection of her fellow performers. "Then, sir," said Nell, "I hope you will make them a handsome present." Charles explained that he did not carry money with him but that he might borrow a few sovereigns from one of his friends. "Odd's fish," said Nell, "what kind of company have I got myself into?"

She was equally quick at repartee when Beck Marshall, a parson's daughter, was foolish enough to call her a whore. "I am a whore to one man," said Nell, "though I was brought up in a bawdy house to fill strong waters to the men : but you are a whore to three or four, though a Presbyter's praying daughter." Pepys considered this answer "very pretty." So was her comment to the king when he brought as a new mistress, Louise de Keroualle from Paris. Nell reminded him albeit in vain that there was an Act of Parliament forbidding the importation of cows from France.

In those days as always when it is a matter of sex, if I may quote Kipling, "The Colonel's lady and Judy O'Grady" were "sisters under the skin." As standards go, Nell Gwynn was more ladylike than the aristocratic Barbara Villiers, the Lady Castlemaine, whom she supplanted in the royal favour. Both could express themselves eloquently in strong language. When Barabara tried to persuade Charles to accept as his son her child by another lover he refused to do so. Barbara stormed into a rage and cried for all the court to hear, "God dammit, you shall own the bastard." In a similar situation, Nell made her point in a much more genteel manner. It was the usual custom of the king to give titles to his illegitimate children. He neglected this duty in the case of his first son by Nell. "Come hither, you little bastard," she said to the boy one day. The king was greatly offended. "What else can I do," said Nell. "I

have no better name to call him." Charles at once created
the boy the Earl of Burford. It was as simple as that.

Let us leave the days of the Stuarts for a while and move
to the Georgian regime, which began in 1714 and ended in
1830. During those 116 years morals in England among rich
and poor had never been lower. The third George was the
only one of the four Hanoverian kings who was willing to
do without a mistress. The aristocrats were as licentious as
their royal masters.

Widespread fornication was the order of the day. Even
the London Stock Exchange had its private brothel. There
were prostitutes at every street corner. Infamous clubs
sprang up overnight like mushrooms. For the benefit of its
members, one of them had printed, *A Whoremonger's
Guide to London.* Jack Harris, an enterprising waiter at
the Shakespeare Hotel near the Strand, issued regularly his
List of Covent Garden Ladies. It may be said that hall
porters in some hotels still will supply visitors with similar
information and telephone numbers.

Jack Harris followed the example of Richard Tattersal,
who opened his London Horse Market at Hyde Park Corner
in 1766 and advertised for sale the best young mares and
stallions. It was as difficult to get on to the books of Jack
Harris as it was to be entered at Tattersal's. Fanny Murray,
who became a most fashionable lady of the town in later
years, was a considerable time in London before she
appeared in the *List of Covent Garden Ladies* as "A Fine
Brown Girl, rising Nineteen next Season."

London was well supplied with experienced procuresses,
constantly on the lookout for buxom young girls fresh from
the country. They would be advertised as "a parson's
daughter" or "a milliner's apprentice." Not far from Covent
Garden there was "A Whore's Initiating School." Every
brothel had its street tout.

It was the charming custom for the mistress of a high
class bordello to call herself "The Abbess" : her pupils were
described as "nuns." These young women were given a
thorough training in the craft of harlotry. One of them
spoke about her initiation more graphically than possibly
any member of her profession could today. "I was but two

days in London," she said, "when I was thrown arsey-varsey into the business."

There was a Shakespearean richness of language then that the Londoner fortunately has not yet lost. Young gallants wrote odes in praise of the charms of their favourite girls. They kept notes of their amorous adventures and could inform their less experienced friends about where their desires could best be satisfied. In "the great wen," as Dr. Johnson called the city, you will find today announcements outside some shops to the effect that "a gentleman can have accommodation in flat where secretarial services are available." It was done more openly in earlier times. In his favourite coffee house a young man would leave a note to inform any applicant that he was anxious to meet "A handsome maid with soft lips and plump bosom who will take delight where she wishes to give it."

The debtors' prisons were a good hunting ground where clerks might find girls in need of money or protection. So was the lunatic asylum at Bedlam. If any unfortunate girl living with imprisoned parents was reluctant to give herself to a lover unless he would offer marriage there was always a parson hovering around St. Paul's who would perform a bogus ceremony for a small consideration.

Many of the clergy were a rum lot. That extraordinary man, John Wilkes, M.P. for the Borough of Aylesbury, wrote to his friend, the Reverend Charles Churchill :

> You should not fail to make yourself known to Effie when you are at Tunbridge Wells. By all means mention my name and you will find her both pliant and pliable. She is gifted with a capacity for translating the language of love into a rich, libidinous and ribald phraseology which lends enchantment to her amoristic acrobatics.

If the Reverend Churchill took this advice when he went to Tunbridge Wells, he was but following the example of a more eminent churchman, Frederick Augustus Hervey, Lord Bishop of Derry and Earl of Bristol, who travelled in state round Europe with a retinue of beautiful women. He became enamoured of the Countess of Lichentau, mistress of Frederick II of Prussia and behaved with her, according to the *Dictionary of National Biography*, "in a manner not worthy of a prince of the Anglican church." That was only one of the interludes this bishop had with the weaker sex, as was testified in her memoirs by his friend, Emma, Lady Hamilton.

This was all part of what Talleyrand called "the sweetness of life." It was an age when the sins of the flesh were all but considered virtues. The horrors of damnation by hell-fire had lost their grip. It was an age when life was desirable for its own sake and many men had ceased to worry about its end.

No wonder that the Victorians were shocked by all they knew and had read about their predecessors. No wonder that sex went underground. No wonder that Charles Dickens and his friend, Wilkie Collins, thought it wiser to find their pleasures more discreetly across the Channel with the grisettes of Paris. No wonder that Dickens kept quiet about his liaison with the lovely little actress, Ellen Ternan, and made his friends believe that he was merely taking a fatherly interest in the girl. If the truth about his private life had been known, few of his worshippers would have believed it. The heroines of the Victorian novelists were all good girls. Not a Moll Flanders, a Fanny Hill nor a "Forever Amber" among them.

The Georgians were at least honest about their sex life. If they were unashamedly bawdy in their talk and public behaviour, they had also dignity and good taste. They chose for themselves the most beautiful mistresses. The lovely Nancy Parsons was immortalised by Gainsborough in a portrait, Kitty Fisher sat for Reynolds. Both were on the Harris *List of Covent Garden Ladies*. Both had London at their feet when Emma Hamilton, painted often by Romney, was barmaid, prostitute and strip-tease girl in "The Temple of Health and Beauty," run by a Scottish doctor at Pall Mall. This was the mecca of all London roués in 1779. The equally attractive Martha Rae, who belonged to the bordello of Catherine Hayes, came to a tragic end when she was shot dead by a love-crazed clergyman outside Covent Garden Theatre.

The first Lord of the English Admiralty, Sir Francis

Dashwood, was said by Horace Walpole to "have fornicated his way all over Europe." Walpole, son of a Prime Minister, was himself a queer bird. There is not any evidence of sexual orgies taking place at the castle he built at Strawberry Hill near Twickenham. But an extraordinary lot of people gathered there. There was Kitty Clive, a retired actress, who according to Lady Townshend had a face like the rising sun. There were dowagers "as plentiful as flounders." There was a mad Irish actor who worked a private printing press and an attorney's wife who was drunk every night and made her servants fire guns from the windows to drive away imaginary men who would wish to rape her. There was also a stuffed tiger. Lady Townshend, who was reputed to have the most scandalous tongue in London, took a poor view of Horace Walpole's masculinity. "The only thing Horace ever wanted to kiss," she said, "is the tiger."

Horace, nevertheless, was a member of the Hell-Fire Club at West Wycombe where lords and dukes and Cabinet Ministers made whoopee with prostitutes sent specially down from London by a notorious brothel keeper, Catherine Hayes. We have a pen picture of the First Lord of the Treasury lying on a couch with one of Mrs. Hayes' young women sitting naked on his stomach. Mrs. Hayes was a colourful character.

She knew all the noble rakes of London. One of her "nuns," Fanny Murray, came into prominence when Wilkes wrote his *Essay on Women*, with the opening line, "Arise my Fanny." This work is considered so indecent that it is kept under lock and key in two London public libraries. It created a sensation when Wilkes was indicted for obscenity and his essay was read in the House of Lords. Some of Fanny's parliamentary lovers were frightened out of their wits in case their names might be mentioned. As it happened, the Earl of Sandwich was the only one who received unfavourable publicity. Everybody in the theatre knew whom John Gay meant in his play, *The Beggars Opera* with the line, "I can't believe that Jeremy Twitcher had peached me." From then on, Sandwich was widely known as Jeremy Twitcher.

It was only to be expected that the writers of the period should be influenced by a society in which profiligacy was such a predominant feature. The morals of Dr. Johnson were beyond reproach but his friend, James Boswell, could always find a frolicsome wench to amuse him for a short time in the dark alleys around Fleet Street and St. Paul's. The great doctor would not have approved of Boswell's tom-cat nocturnal diversions any more than he did when he wrote about Lord Buckhurst and his friends getting drunk at the Cock Tavern in Fleet Street:

> Going into the balcony they exposed themselves in very indecent postures. At last one of them stood forth naked and harangued the crowd in such profane language that the public indignation was awakened: the crowd attempted to force the door and being repulsed drove in the performers with stones and broke the windows of the house.

Andrew Marvell, poet and M.P. for Hull, was as much incensed as Johnson when he drew up a list of parliamentary abuses. Among them were the unrefuted allegations that Sir Winston Churchill, father of the future Duke of Marlborough, was "a pimp" and that Sir George Downing, M.P. for Weymouth, "kept six whores in pay."

Members of Parliament were clearly of no higher moral rectitude than the actors of the period who, because of their way of life, might have been excused when they strayed from the straight and narrow path. Yet Edmund Kean, the greatest tragedian of his day, was driven from the stage because of an unfortunate affair with the wanton wife of a London alderman. In his letters to her he called her "His Darling Little Breeches." The court case that ensued caused as much of a sensation as the legal squabble about *Lady Chatterley's Lover* did in our time.

Neither the public nor his creditors had mercy on young George Farquhar, actor, brilliant writer of comedy and clergyman's son. In spite of being constantly in debt, he was able to maintain three mistresses at one time. His play *Beaux Stratagem* is as great a classic as Sheridan's *The School for Scandal*. Both reflect the vices and follies of their periods. Both men were dying in poverty when the bailiffs were knocking on their door. Both might have said, as Sir

Thomas Beecham did when he heard that his affairs were being put in the hands of the Official Receiver of Bankruptcy : "May the Lord make him truly thankful for what he is about to receive."

The writers of those years made full use of the material they found ready to their hand. Defoe took his *Robinson Crusoe* from the true story of a Scottish seaman, Alexander Selkirk, who was marooned on the island of Juan Ferdandez in the Pacific. His *Moll Flanders* could have been any one of a hundred girls he saw each day around Newgate prison or his father's butcher's shop at Cripplegate. John Cleland, a dissolute ex-member of the British Consular Service would have had little trouble finding a model for his *Fanny Hill or the Memoirs of a Woman of Pleasure*.

In 1750 when Cleland wrote his book, there was a "Society for the Reclamation of Fallen Women." They must have had a thankless job. Women like Moll Flanders and Fanny Hill were falling like ninepins all around them. Fanny Murray, a flower seller from Bath, was seduced when she was fourteen by Jack Spencer, favourite nephew of the Duchess of Marlborough. Fanny Hill, also from the country, fell when she was fifteen. Like Fanny Murray, she made her way to London and soon found herself under the roof of "Mother Brown." Those who have read Cleland's book will know his heroine went from one lover to another. Her career as a prostitute is almost identical with the real life story of Fanny Murray.

Cleland, whose own story is a sordid tale of depravity, knew well the brothels of London and other cities abroad where he had been a highly placed British civil servant. He wrote his book to make money to satisfy his insatiable craving for drink and women. He sold the manuscript outright to a publisher for eighteen pounds. It was the rage of London when it appeared towards the end of the reign of George II in serial form. John Cleland had made his story lurid enough. Greater slices of pornography were inserted in numerous editions by the publisher, who had the not inappropriate name of Drybutter. That most reliable fountain of information, *The Dictionary of National Biography*, may be quoted again for the statement that Mr. Drybutter made himself £10,000, a colossal sum in those days, out of his investment of eighteen pounds.

Wiser in this respect than Cleland was Ned Ward, whose name is known only now to students of London history. Not for him the scandals of royalty, noblemen and Members of Parliament. As his own publisher he wrote mainly about the vices of the ordinary people, the Billingsgate fishwives, the Thames watermen, the frequenters of the lower ale-houses and taverns. You will read much more about him later in this book. Unlike Cleland, Defoe and Fielding, who wrote *Joseph Andrews* and *Tom Jones*, Ward has never been republished since his death in 1731.

The strange thing is that we know practically nothing about Ned Ward's private life, except that he was a poet, a publican and a pamphleteer and, like Horace Walpole, a great retailer of gossip. Walpole recorded that when friends of his went to see Sir Henry Fielding they found this distinguished author at supper eating "cold mutton and a ham bone with a whore and three Irishmen." Ward is equally graphic about the lovemaking, eating and drinking customs of lesser mortals.

This chapter is merely a prologue to a story in which there may well be many similarities to the vices and follies of our own century. The curtain is about to rise. The first scene is set in the days of good Queen Anne.

2

IN QUEEN ANNE'S TIME

> Our story a secret! Lord help you. Go out and tell 'em—
> Queen Anne's dead.

There were roars of laughter in the theatre when an actor spoke those lines in George Colman's comedy, *The Heir-at-Law*, in the year 1790. The reason was that by then Queen Anne had been dead for the most of a hundred years. Thus came into the English language an expression which has lasted ever since.

If less has been written about Anne than most English queens, it is not because her background was unromantic. Her story begins with the execution of her grandmother, the lovely Mary Stuart, Queen of Scots. When her son, James, died, the unfortunate Charles I, succeeded him as king. One of his most faithful adherents was Edward Hyde, grandfather of Queen Anne. "I must make Ned Hyde my Secretary of State," the king wrote, "for the truth is I can trust no other."

This same Ned Hyde, whose name is commemorated in London's most famous park, became one of the most influential men in England. When she was twenty-two, his daughter, Anne, married James Stuart, the second son of Charles I. Their daughter, another Anne, in the direct line of Stuart succession, was to become the future queen of England. These facts are intended only to put right the historical record and show how Anne came to spend her girlhood in the highly immoral court of her uncle, Charles II.

Anne's reign for her was not particularly happy. Her husband, George, Prince of Denmark, a kindly good-natured man, who had been chosen for her by Uncle Charles, was completely out of place at court. "I have tried

George drunk, and I have tried George sober," said the king, "and there is nothing to him." Charles had little use for anybody who wasn't interested in seducing women. George preferred the bottle. He was not Anne's only worry. She had a formidable lifetime enemy in Sarah Jennings, Duchess of Marlborough, who had been her playmate at Court when they were children. There was a mutual dislike. Ann was plain, quiet and virtuous. Sarah was vivacious, attractive and lewd.

In her later years, she kept statesmen, soldiers, even her husband and her mother, completely under her thumb. When her mother, who was something of a termagant herself, found St. James's Palace a haven to escape from her creditors, there was a family row. Mrs. Jennings was politely asked to leave. Her answer was that she would do so and "By the grace of God she would take her daughter with her, as two maids had great bellies at court." She didn't want her daughter, who was fourteen at the time, to be with child so young. This maternal thoughtfulness was not appreciated. The upset was that mother and daughter came to blows. Young Sarah told the king bluntly that she would leave the palace if her mother was not forcibly removed. The dominant young woman got her way.

On November 23, 1676, this information appeared in the Belvoir manuscripts :

> Sarah Jennings has got the best of her mother, who is commanded to leave the court, and her daughter in it, the girl saying her mother is a madwoman.

So Sarah remained at court, to become the Duchess of Marlborough and the plague of Anne's existence. She knew there the two earls, Rochester and Buckingham, whose full stories you will hear later. Charles had learned a lot about the pursuit of women when Buckingham was in exile with him at the French court. It was Buckingham who introduced his protege to Cousin Barbara, the Lady Castlemaine.

Out of her bedroom window one morning, Charles saw young John Churchill, quietly creeping out. Charles knew that Barbara had been keeping this youthful lover well supplied with money. He packed young Churchill, later to become the great Duke of Marlborough, off to Tangier, with this kindly farewell :

"I forgive you, for you did it for your bread."

These were surely the words of a magnanimous man. I like to think of them as true and not backstairs tittle-tattle as so many court stories undoubtedly were. There were always servants only too willing to supply spicy chit-chat to the gossip gatherers. The greatest of all these, Samuel Pepys, through the grapevine got the news that "the King spent bonfire night with Lady Castlemaine and did send for a pair of scales and they did weigh each other."

There is a delightful domestic scene to imagine—Charles and the beautiful Barbara, her long dark auburn hair falling down to her hips weighing each other in soft candle-light as the bonfires glowed outside in Whitehall. Full marks must go to Pepys as the retailer of exclusive information. Very little escaped that furtive prying mind.

He was able to reveal that one evening at the theatre Lady Castlemaine wore jewels worth £40,000 and that she lost half that amount of money playing cards. He knew better than any modern crime reporter all about the marauding clubs, later to be known as the Mohocks, who wrecked one night all the brothels in the centre of London, not because they disapproved of such establishments but just for hellery. He knew about the anonymous publication of a pamphlet sent to Barbara and entitled, *The Poor Whore's Petition to the Most Splendid Illustrious, Serene and Eminent Lady of Pleasure, the Lady Castlemaine*. All these women were asking for was protection permitting them to carry on their trade with as much freedom as their more privileged sisters at court.

One of the court beauties, "La Belle Hamilton," was in a position to supply first-hand information to her husband, Le Compte Philibert de Grammont, who wrote this account of royal junketings on the Thames :

'Twas from the stairs of the Place at Whitehall that the Court took to the Water, towards the close of those summer days when dust and heat did not permit walking in St. James's

Park. An infinite number of open boats full of celebrated
Beauties of the Court and Citie attended the Barges, in which
were the Royal family: and Colations, Musick and Fireworks
completed the entertainment.

When Charles died there came the short reign of Anne's
father, James II, who fled from England to France after
his defeat by William, Prince of Orange, at the Battle of
the Boyne, still celebrated annually in Ireland. William had
married Anne's sister, Mary, a gushing, fatuous woman
who, according to Sarah Jennings, had "no bowels." She
was foolish enough to believe that a man so ugly as William
would not follow the royal custom and get himself a mistress. She obviously knew little about the highly sexed
women of the Villiers' family when she took Barbara Castlemaine's cousin Betty into her household as a maid of
honour. In an effort to gain as much power over the new
king as Cousin Barbara had over Charles, Betty soon en-
ticed William to her bedroom.

When Mary's suspicions were aroused, she trailed
William one night through the corridors of Kensington
Palace and found him engaged in what must have been
one of the most unromantic of all royal love affairs. The
king, "the Little Dutchman," as the English called him,
had a parrot nose and was entirely without charm. There
was a scene such as Kensington Palace had not seen before
or possibly since. Miss Villiers had to pack her bags and
go. Sarah Jennings carried the news to Anne, who had
never liked her sister or her husband. No woman loved re-
tailing gossip more than Sarah Jennings. She had a delightful trick when she was losing control of the conversation of
putting her toe under the table and sending the teacups
sprawling over the floor. Then with a charming smile she
would say, "I'm sorry—just an accident."

Mary never forgave William for this indiscretion. His
lapse with Betty Villiers seems to have been his one and
only affair with women. It soon, however, became common
knowledge that he was a homosexual. From Holland he had
brought with him a handsome young man, Joost van
Keppel, and made him Earl of Albemarle. Keppel, a brilliant administrator, was a rake who managed to keep his

private life a secret. He maintained a handsome brunette as his mistress in Chelsea, but there were two sides to his character and he was undoubtedly effeminate. There were connecting doors between his room and the royal chamber at Kensington. Betty Villiers had gone and Mary was dead. Although there is little evidence of this on paper, the rumour has persisted through the years that William and his chief adviser were consenting adults in sodomy. The king died after falling from his horse when it tripped over a mole hill as he was riding from Hampton Court. The favourite toast of his enemies, the Jacobites, who wanted another Stuart on the throne, was "Here's to the little gentleman in the velvet coat."

When Anne became queen in 1702, there was another Stuart on the throne. The people thought there would be a merry England once again. But life at Anne's court was neither so immoral or so gay as it had been during the reign of Uncle Charles. One thing, however, remained unchanged. Rakery and bawdiness if anything increased. The brothel-keepers, who had been slightly suppressed during the reign of William and Mary, began again to reap a rich harvest.

But bawdy houses there had always been in London. A much more violent and dangerous form of vice was now rampant. The streets were made unsafe at night for both men and women by gangs of young men who had formed themselves into clubs with the fearsome names of "The Scourers," "The Roaring Boys," "The Bravados," "The Roysters" and "The Mohocks." The few men of "the Watch," whose duty it was to safeguard the freedom and lives of the citizens, were completely unable to deal with this new wave of crime. The gallants and their lady friends coming from the theatres around Covent Garden were specially selected as the victims. But it was not only a war of class distinction. Many of the club members belonged to the middle and upper classes. Swift was of the opinion that young Thomas Burnet, son of Bishop Burnet, belonged to "The Mohocks." This, the most outrageous of all the clubs, was believed to be supported by the Whig party as an embarrasment to the Tories then in power. The reput-

able writers of the period unanimously condemned the
gangs. In *The Spectator* for March 12, 1712, two years
before Anne's death, Steele had this to say about the terrori-
sation of the streets of London :

> One of the offices of the gangs is to set up women on their
> heads and commit certain indecencies on them. I forbear to
> mention these acts, because they could not but be very shocking
> to my readers. This is a war against mankind. By the standard
> maxim of their policy, they enter into no alliance but one:
> and that is offensive and defensive against all bawdy houses,
> of which they declare themselves both protectors and
> guarantors.

Steele's full account of these outrages might well have
been written about the protection rackets of our own day.
Unlike Uncle Charles, who couldn't have cared less, or her
brother-in-law, William, who was too busy with his own
sexual abnormality, Anne was worried about the increase
of vice in the streets of her capital city. On March 17, 1712,
she had an edict published to the effect that "Great and
Unusual Riots and Barbarities have been committed in the
Night-Time in the Open Streets by Numbers of Evil-
Disposed Persons." An award of a hundred pounds was
offered to any person who would tell who the ringleaders
were and turn Queen's evidence against them. This royal
decree brought no beneficial result. Any informer who had
the necessary information knew what would have happened
to him if he had claimed the money. The underworld of
London was even more callous than it is today.

Anne was sincere in her desire to bring about reform and
see justice done. She took a personal interest in the behaviour of a colonel in her Horse Guards, a villain unique
in the annals of the British army. He had begun a life of
crime and seduction during the reign of Uncle Charles. He
reached the apex of his rakery when Anne was queen.
Charles, if he had known him, would probably have created
him a belted earl. Anne made it her business to see that he
was cashiered from the army. The indictments against him
were numerous. Each time he escaped by the payment of
a fine.

On April 15, 1725, Sarah Seletto, a young woman from

the country, told Mr. Justice Ellis at Pall Mall that she had been decoyed by a Mrs. Pratt to a house in New Bond Street and raped there by a colonel. Sarah Wilkins testified that she had succumbed to the colonel under threat and on payment of a guinea and had later borne him a child. He had told her that his name was Hornby. On each of his appearances in court the colonel got off as lightly as if he had been charged with a minor motoring offence today.

The real name of the notorious colonel was Francis Charteris. If he is selected as an example of the rakes of the Queen Anne period, it is not because there were not many like him but because he is in his own sphere incomparable. Anne first heard of the colonel's exploits through Sarah Jennings. It was a case of the pot calling the kettle blackface. The morals of the Duchess of Marlborough were not beyond reproach but this didn't worry Sarah Jennings. Her Duke, who had first known the delights of Venus with Barbara Castlemaine when he was young John Churchill was certainly not a paragon of virtue. It came to his notice that Colonel Charteris was not behaving like an officer and a gentleman. He promptly had him arrested. On November 3, 1711, Anne put an end to the colonel's military career by appointing Lord James Murray to take over the command of her Horse Guards. This setback, however, did not have any serious effect on a man who was born to be a rake.

Lord Macaulay in a famous passage from his works wrote about the most dissolute of all Frenchmen, Bertrand Barère :

> Barère approached nearer than any person mentioned in history or fiction, whether man or devil, to the idea of consummate and universal depravity. In him the proper objects of hatred and contempt preserve an exquisite and absolute harmony. In almost every sort of wickedness he has not a rival. His sensuality was immoderate : but that is a failing common to many great and amiable men. There have been many men as cowardly, some as cruel, a few as mean, a few as impudent. There may also have been as many great liars. But when we put everything together, sensuality, poltroonery, baseness, effrontery, mendacity, barbarity, the result is something which in a novel we should condemn as a caricature.

Those are hard words, Lord Macaulay, but you might as well have written them about Colonel Francis Charteris, whose full story would need a book in itself. It can only here be brieflly summarised. He was born in 1675, the son of a wealthy landowner, Sir John Charteris of Amisfield. As a young man he was given a commission in the Horse Guards. After his father's death he inherited property and an income of some £100,000 a year. In 1701, he was drummed out of the army for cheating at cards. When England needed men to fight her wars, he rejoined and saw service in Flanders. He was drummed out of the army again for stealing a large piece of beef in a butchers' shambles at Bruges. One would wonder why a wealthy young man would wish to do this. But truth in the story of Francis Charteris is much stranger than fiction. He was a coward who could always extricate himself from fighting a duel when challenged. He was an absentee during the battle of Blenheim. On August 24, 1701, eleven days after Blenheim, this notice appeared in the *Army Gazette*.

> One Charteris, an officer in the army, is suspended for having had the impudence to place himself at the Commander's table and when he was turned out to draw upon the gentleman who was commanded to do it.

Back in England he preferred not to look after his estates but devote his time to cheating at cards and seducing country girls. When a pretty chambermaid entered his bedroom in a Lancaster inn, he offered her a guinea if she would spend the night with him. After threats the girl agreed. In the morning, having lost most of his money gambling the previous day, he was unable to pay his bill. He told the landlord that the chambermaid had robbed him. The guinea was found in her possession, she was dismissed from her job and Charteris went gaily off. He was remembered for years afterwards as "the man who betrayed the servant girl and robbed her of her earnings."

One incident of this kind followed another. While he was in the act of raping the young wife of a miller near Edinburgh, the husband appeared, overpowered him and had him arrested. The following news item appeared in *Fog's Weekly Journal* for December 28, 1728:

We hear a Colonel is charged with rape, a misfortune that he has been liable to, but for which he has not yet been prosecuted.

The name of Francis Charteris appeared frequently in the scurrilous pamphlets of the time. In one of them he was referred to as "The Great Rake-Master of England." He spent most of his time in the London gambling dens, taverns and brothels.

Contemporary drawings show Charteris as a leering debauched character with a cruel and bitter face. Hogarth portrayed him in Plate 1 of *The Harlot's Progress*. The young country girl, "Moll Hackabout," is being accosted on the street by "the old Baud," Mother Bentley, while the colonel stands waiting in the background. Beside Charteris is his man, Gourlay, whose job it was to lure girls into the colonel's London home at Poland Street on the promise that they would be employed there as maid. This plan worked well for a number of years. Then one young woman having been forced at pistol point to fall in with the master's desires escaped and laid still another indictment against him. The case was duly tried and this verdict reached:

The Proceedings at the Sessions for the Peace of the Citie of London, held at Justice Hall at the Old Bailey on Friday, before the Rt. Honourable Sir Richard Brocas, Knight, Lord Mayor of London, the Honourable Mr. Justice Price and Mr. Justice Probyn: upon a Bill of Indictment found against Francis Charteris, Esq., for committing a rape on the body of Anne Bond, of which he was found guilty.

On April 10, 1730, at a meeting of the Privy Council, George II, who was an authority on rakery and seduction, gave the colonel a King's Pardon. If Anne had been on the throne, Charteris, who carried on his life of depravity till he was fifty-seven, might well have finished up on the gallows at Tyburn. But Anne was dead.

Her life had not been particularly happy. For months before her death she had been suffering from quaking fits and attacks of gout. On her last appearances in public her face was so covered with blotches that she had to have it painted.

It was rumoured that she had followed the example of

her consort and taken to the bottle, that she never drank tea unless it was well laced with brandy. In those days the populace knew more about the private lives of the royal family than they do today. The women of Billingsgate and the Thames watermen called out "Old Brandy Face" at Anne as she sailed down the river in the royal barge. It is true that Anne ate too much and drank more than was good for her. Sarah Jennings said that "the Queen never went beyond such a quantity of strong drink as her doctors thought necessary." It was, however, admitted that Anne kept "Vials of Penny Royal Water in her Closet."

The comedian, W. C. Fields, to fortify himself during rehearsals, had in his dressing room a flask of gin weakly diluted with pineapple juice. When somebody emptied the flask and filled it with pure pineapple juice, W. C. Fields took a sip, spat it out and asked : "Who's been putting pineapple juice in my pineapple juice?" It may well be that now and then Sarah Jennings put some "Penny Royal Water" into Queen Anne's "Penny Royal Water."

3

THE EARL RAKES

These Earls were worthy men.

The ancient Celtic chronicler who wrote those words was referring to "The Flight of the Earls," an important occasion in Irish history. His two earls, Hugh O'Neill, Earl of Tyrone, and Rory O'Donnel, Earl of Tirconnail, fled from Donegal because they were—or thought they were—in danger of being slaughtered by the English invaders. They spent the remainder of their lives on the Continent, brawling, drinking and riotously living. They had almost as roistering a time there as two English earls had when they fled from London many years later.

The Irish chieftains went to Italy and France for their spree. The two English noblemen got only as far as Newmarket. Their intention was not to have a flutter on the horses which is the normal reason why people go to a famous racecourse. The Duke of Buckingham and his friend, the Earl of Rochester, had different ideas. They travelled to Newmarket for the purpose of seducing there as many attractive young women as possible. Their unqualified success in this venture is the most remarkable story of licentious rake-hellery that can be found in English fact or fiction. It would be incredible if we had not proof of it from Archbishop Burnet, who wrote a life of Rochester. Not even Colonel Charteris could have conceived such a plan for mass seduction.

The colonel would have gone about the job like a bull charging a gate. The two noblemen of this story knew better. To their credit it must be said that they carried out the manoeuvre in a most generous and gentlemanly manner. No pistol-point rapery or the use of brute force for them—just charm, a little money, plenty of good food and lashings and leavings of good drink. It is possible that many people in Newmarket were sorry to see them leave. Rochester certainly left behind one broken-hearted beauty who could well have been the rustic Corinna of some of his most amorous poems.

It is doubtful if two more dedicated rakes ever lived than these two friends of Queen Anne's Uncle Charles. Both were endowed with silver tongues, both were most handsome men. Buckingham, judged by his portrait by Rubens, was a swashbuckling type with a close resemblance to Errol Flynn. He shocked some of his more pious friends by "winking and smiling at comely and beautiful women at Divine service." He had as we say today "an eye for the girls." We know from the archives of the House of Stuart that "George Villiers, Duke of Buckingham, was responsible for the fall from virtue of more than one beautiful maiden." But these were ladies of the court and not the fresh rosy-cheeked wenches of Newmarket. Buckingham, we are told, "looked upon the whole race of women as inferior beings." He delighted in telling stories of the many happy moments he had spent "in the arms of wanton beauties."

His friend, Rochester, was a different type, pale, romantic with Byronic good looks, a man who could woo almost any woman with his soft voice and flattery. He was also no mean poet who wrote lyrical odes in praise of the charms of Venus. Many of them are without doubt the most pornographic in the English language. It is strange that while the obscene verse of John Wilkes is kept under lock and key at the British Museum the much more erotic works of Rochester can be taken from a shelf and read in any of the larger London libraries. Rochester wrote unashamedly about sex. As he said himself his love lyrics were not intended to be set to music and sung as anthems in the Royal chapel. He composed them mainly to amuse his friends at court.

"Rochester's love poems," wrote his biographer, "are too obscene for ladies' eyes but they have their peculiar beauty." But the eyes of many ladies, not only at court but in the homes of London aldermen and the coffee shops and bawdy houses, eagerly read all that Rochester wrote or was supposed to have written. His verses were the common property of servants and more exalted people in the palace at White-hall. When a new piece appeared it was sold to a printer who added obscenities of his own to make it spicier reading for the ordinary Londoners who were always interested in the scandals of their betters. One of the king's lesser known mistresses, Moll Davis, who knew the stewpots well, re-ported that verses "by my Lord Rochester are being cry'd in the streets."

Like Buckingham, Rochester had many affairs with the ladies of the court. Most of them were frightened by the lighthearted wickedness of his tongue. Very few, not even the king nor Nell Gwynn, escaped this. A good mixer if ever there was one, Rochester shared his favours equally with the titled ladies and the household staff. A lesbian overseer in the kitchen gave this advice to a pretty house-maid in whom she was interested:

> Don't go within reaching distance of my Lord Rochester. Not a girl in the palace who gives her ear to him but loses her virginity.

One such girl, however, owed her future success to Rochester. He seduced Elizabeth Barry, who attended one of the court ladies and who was recognised everywhere as a beauty. After she had borne him a child, he paid for her education in music and dramatic art. When she was a little over twenty he got her an engagement to play at Covent Garden. Her talent and good looks did not go long without recognition. She lived to become one of the greatest actresses of her time.

Before attempting to understand the reason for the New-market flight of the earls, it is necessary to know something about the hazards of being a courtier. Rochester's main contribution to life at Whitehall was the writing of obscene verse. Buckingham was both a soldier and a diplomat. Be-cause of a family friendship with the king, he was brought up at the royal court of Charles. He owned large properties and had an income of £26,000 a year. He was believed then to be the richest nobleman in England.

The king called him "Steenie" and considered him his

best adviser on affairs of state and finding suitable mistresses. One of these was a member of his own family, Barbara Villiers, the Lady Castlemaine of later years. We first hear of her in royal circles in the diary of Pepys. She was then plain Mrs. Palmer.

> Great doings of music in the next house, which was Whalleys. The King and the Dukes were there with Madame Palmer, a pretty woman they hold a fancy to and to make her husband a cuckold.

This was a merry party at the Whalleys. There was a kind of parlour game of hide and seek, with one or other of the dukes "talking very wantonly" to Mrs. Palmer, as she coyly played peek-a-boo with them and popped in and out behind curtains. It was only to be expected that her favours went to the king. Mr. Palmer faded from the scene. Charles created him Lord Castlemaine right away. It was as easy as that. Buckingham was now firmly in control.

He was made Master of the King's Horse. Pepys wrote, "The Duke of Buckingham do rule all now." Some trouble arose when the duke cast his eye on the lovely Countess of Shrewsbury and had to fight a duel with her husband, who died from the wounds received. Buckingham took up residence with the countess and was forgiven by the king after he had found him another mistress, "La Belle Stuart," the loveliest girl at court. When Charles boasted to his friends that she had the most shapely legs in Europe, "La Belle Stuart" obediently lifted her skirt to prove that the king was right.

Buckingham was a perfect mimic. Miss Stuart went into fits of giggles at his impersonations of important people in court circles, especially those he didn't like or who didn't like him. He had a trying time keeping the peace between his Cousin Barbara and "La Belle Stuart," a childish creature who loved dressing dolls and building castles with cards. The king before she fled worshipped her. He was so infatuated with her playfulness that he would cuddle her at every possible moment and dandle her on his knee.

This was not to the liking of Lady Castlemaine. Miss Stuart had been painted by Sir Peter Lely. By the king's desire she sat as the model for Britannia on the new coins about to be minted. Barbara, no doubt taking advice from Cousin Buckingham, decided that if she couldn't beat "La Belle Stuart" she would join her. She went out of her way to become her rival's friend. For first-hand information, we must go again to Pepys:

> Lady Castlemaine, a few days since, had Miss Stuart to an entertainment, and at night began a frolic that they two must be married: and married they were, with ring and all other ceremonies of church service, and ribbons with a sack posset in bed, and flinging the stocking: but in the close, it is said that my Lady Castlemaine, who was the bridegroom, rose from the bed and the King got in and took her place.

Charles did not always trust his friend, "Steenie," who played many a double game. Louis XIV used him as a spy, paid him £10,000 a year and presented him with a golden snuff box set with diamonds. On more than one occasion Charles sent "Steenie" to cool himself in the Tower of London.

When Lady Castlemaine constantly pleaded for his release, Charles called her a whore, a not uncommon occurrence among these royal lovers. The king when he got over his bad temper always relented under feminine pressure. And after all the court was often dull without a court jester. About Buckingham, John Dryden wrote:

> A man so various that he seemed to be
> Not one but all mankind's epitome.
> And in the course of one revolving moon
> Was chemist, fiddler, statesman and buffoon.

In his office as a statesman, Buckingham spent much time in France, where he set many feminine hearts a flutter. Let me quote from his biographer, M. A. Gibb:

> To the casual observer it seemed that his whole object was to dazzle a court well accustomed to splendour with his presence. His famous white satin suit, magnificently studded with diamonds, took the French courtiers by storm. The tall handsome Englishman.... From the moment of his arrival one lady at least, of very high rank, was more than willing to forget her husband For Buckingham had captured the girlish

The Sculptors part is done the features hitt
of Ma: am Gwin No Arte can shew her Witt,

P. lely Pinxit.   G. Valck Sculp: & ex:

Plate *i* "Pretty, witty, sweet NELL GWYN."

Plate 3 JOHN MONTAGU, 4th Earl of Sandwich, in the costume of The Divan Club.

Plate 2 KITTY FISHER "The most pretty, extravagant, wicked little whore who ever flourished."

imagination of no less a person than the Queen of France, the pleasure-loving Anne.... One evening in June, Buckingham was walking with Anne in the beautiful gardens of her palace. As they strolled down a lovely avenue, the magic of the soft moonlight provided a setting for a love scene. They were alone and he began to whisper impetuous words of passion to the Queen.

Anne was only too ready to accept Buckingham as a lover. Before long he had access to her bedroom. Is it any wonder that this Lothario and his Don Juan like friend, Rochester, wrought havoc among the women of Newmarket.

In most respects, Rochester was a more interesting character than Buckingham. By his own merit he got his degree of Master of Arts at Oxford when he was fourteen. Maybe that should be a lesson—or maybe an incentive—to any young freshman who aspires to be a Rochester, who expressed his philosophy by saying "The Three Businesses of this Age are Women, Drinking and Politicks." With politics a bad third, Rochester became expert in the other two recreations. After a tour of the Continent, he returned to London and was warmly accepted at court as a wit, a story teller and a writer of obscenities. Much of what he wrote was like something you would see today scribbled on a lavatory wall. His *Extemporary Words to a Postboy* are unprintable for widespread reading in book form. He took an undergraduate delight in offering Charles verses like "Every Young Maid's Wish."

> A Knight delights in deeds of arms,
> Perhaps a lady loves sweet music's charms.
> Rich men in store of wealth delighted be
> Infants love dandling on their mother's knee.
> Coy maids love something which I'll not express.
> Keep the first letters of these lines and guess.

Before we condemn Rochester for this boyish ribaldry, let us remember that Shakespeare often wrote in similar vein. There are lines in his *Romeo and Juliet*, which might even today produce one or two maidenly blushes if spoken in a school performance, as when Mercutio tells Romeo :

The bawdy hand of the clock is on the prick of noon.

2—THR

Or when this same Mercutio addresses Romeo in the same play :

> I conjure thee by Rosaline's bright eyes,
> By her high forehead and her scarlet lips,
> By her fine foot, her legs and quivering thighs,
> And the demesne that there adjacent lies.

Do those lines not compare with Rochester's ode to his Corinna ?

> In a silent shady grove,
> Fit for the delights of love,
> On Corinna's breast I lay.
> Playing with Et Ceterae.
> Thus the moment passed away,
> Playing with Et Ceterae.
> Her innocence was not betrayed
> No opposition had she made.
> She hugged me close, again did say.
> 'Once more my love—Et Ceterae.'

The king enjoyed this kind of verse and delighted telling stories about Rochester's adventures. Again we must go to Pepys :

And here saw all the people and heard the silly discourses of the King, with his people about him, telling a story of my Lord Rochester's having lost his clothes, while he was with a wench: and his gold all gone, but his clothes found afterwards, stuffed in a feather bed by the wench who stole them.

When Charles found some of the filthiest lines of all written beneath a picture of Nell Gwynn, he had Rochester arrested and sent to the Tower. He spent the time there planning more of his fanciful ideas. It was said that Charles used the Tower as a kind of rest home for Buckingham and Rochester from where they would return to court refreshed.

On one occasion when Buckingham and Rochester were unwelcome at court, they left London in search of new amorous experience. Knowing that the king often visited Newmarket, they went there. On previous visits to the town, they had observed many attractive girls and women in and around the neighbourhood. They carried their pitchers to the pumps, they worked in the fields making hay and sat sunning themselves on their doorsteps. The two noblemen had chosen glorious warm weather for their journey. John Hayward, who has given a full acount of the seduction at Newmarket, wrote in his introduction to the collected poems of Rochester :

> They considered not whether they were maids, wives nor widows but decided to seduce them all.

With their purses well lined with sovereigns, Buckingham and Rochester took possession of an inn for their private use for an indefinite period. The landlord being well paid had no objection and was only too willing to co-operate. In full control of the inn, the two noblemen invited young and old in the town to be their guests and to eat and drink and make merry to their heart's content. The one condition was that the womenfolk should be dressed in the best of their finery and add glamour to the festivities.

On the first evening, the inn and the green fields around were like a Bartholomew Fair. The men drank till they were speechless and the selected women were so happy that they made little resistance to the approaches of the two gentlemen from London and needed little cajolery or enticement to visit them in their private rooms. When the love-making was over, Buckingham sang and mimicked to the accompaniment of fiddles. Rochester entertained the company by reciting his bawdy verse. Few if any of the most desirable women could refuse anything to these handsome and genial hosts. There was one exception.

Rochester had seen from a distance the most beautiful woman in the town, the buxom young wife of a wealthy and miserly landowner. Fearful of losing her and his money, the husband had both guarded day and night by his servants and his maiden sister. The young wife was not permitted to attend the parties, in spite of cordial invitations. Rochester had seldom before been so stricken by the beauty of a young woman. He arranged with Buckingham to invite the old man to supper. Then, as Byron's Don Juan did when he gained his entry to a harem, he dressed as a woman and went to the house with a liberal supply of wine, to which, he had heard, the maiden sister was addicted.

He was refused admittance by the servants. He fell groaning in a swoon on the doorstep. Hearing the commotion, the young woman enquired what was wrong. With sympathy for one of her own sex and glad of any company, she gave instructions that the girl should be brought indoors. Rochester came out of his fainting fit and persuaded the old lady to drink some wine. It was so heavily drugged that she fell fast asleep.

Alone with the young wife, Rochester took off his women's clothes and stood before her as a fairy prince she might have often dreamed about. She was so delighted with his manners and appearance that she readily yielded to his embraces. They went out happily into the moonlight and hid behind a hedge as they watched the husband staggering home from the inn. She was his Corinna of the silent shady groves. She found ways of meeting him on her daily walks and lay in his arms in the heat of those summer days. He told how she had given him "many transports of joy" while he remained in Newmarket.

But even the idyllic lovemaking had to end. Knowing that the king was coming to the races, his two friends went to meet him. He received them with open arms. They took him to their inn and found him "a pretty whore." There were many sad girls in Newmarket when the two noblemen returned to London and what, to Rochester at least, may have been the lesser pleasures of the royal court.

None of the rakes whose stories will be told later in this book were so accomplished in making love and pleasing women as Rochester. He was a man for all seasons. He would dress sometimes as a workman and go wenching in the city slums. He kidnapped a wealthy heiress at Charing Cross from her coach and married her. Calling himself Alexander Bendo, he set up as a quack at Tower Hill and sold beauty preparations and cures for all ailments. Court ladies borrowed dresses from their maids and went to consult him. His publicity placard would have done credit to any modern advertising agent :

Those who have seen French and Spanish women will tell you what Art can do to assist Nature in the Preservation of Beauty. In these countries, Women of forty bear the same

Complexion of a Girl of fifteen: whereas in England, look a Horse in the Mouth and a Woman in her Face and you know their ages to a year.

Rochester was a leading member of a club called "The Ballers," the most mischievous set of young men and women who ever met together. Pepys is our authority for proof of this statement :

> To company in an Arbor—and here I first understood the nature of a club called "The Ballers," Howles telling me how it was a meeting of young blades when he was among them and my Lady Bennett and her Ladies: and there was dancing naked: and all the roguish things in the world.

For the use of the male members of this club, Rochester had imported from France a consignment of "leather appliances." Nothing is known about how these articles were used but it would seem that they were worn by the young men to give greater satisfaction to the ladies. Their shape aroused suspicion and curiosity among the Customs' officials at Dover. Rochester was told by a friend at Whitehall in a letter that an Act of Parliament of 1673 forbade importation of certain French goods. The upshot of this story is that the wives of the Customs' officials took possession of the entire consignment.

In the British Museum there is a record of "a freak which my Lord Rochester and some lady friends committed on the Sabbath."

> During that day they ran along Woodstock Road naked. When chidded that he had stripped himself of both his prudence and his breeches, Rochester replied that they had gone into the river and had a frisk in the meadow to dry themselves.

He was thirty-three when he died, comforted by his faithful friend, Bishop Burnet. He had few, if any, enemies. Buckingham had few, if any, friends. He was sixty-six when he died in a small Yorkshire tavern. Pope wrote his epitaph :

> In the worst inn's worst room, with mat half hung,
> The floors of plaster and the walls of dung,
> The George and Garter dangling from the bed,
> Where tawdry yellow strove with dirty red,
> Great Villiers lies: alas, how changed from him,

That life of pleasure and that soul of whim.
No wit to flatter left in all his store,
No fool to laugh at which he valued more
Bereft of health, of fortune and of friends,
And fame, this lord of useless thousands ends.

So died the richest and at one time the most powerful
man in England.

4

THE GEORGIAN YEARS

> I sing the Georges Four,
> For Providence could stand no more.
> Some say that far the worst
> Of all was George the First.
> But yet by some 'tis reckoned
> That worser still was George the Second:
> And what mortal ever heard
> Any good of George the Third.
> When George the Fourth from Earth descended,
> Thank God, the reign of Georges ended.

Walter Savage Landor wrote those lines in an idle moment when he was not engaged in more serious composition. There is, nevertheless, substantial truth in what he thought of the four Georges, who occupied the throne of England for the most of a hundred years. Daniel Defoe wrote of the first George :

> This royal refugee our blood restores
> With foreign courtiers and foreign whores,
> And carefully repeopled us again
> Throughout his lazy long lascivious reign.

As a Hanoverian, George I did not speak nor did he make any effort to learn English. He swore like a trooper in his own language at his German mistresses, two women whom his subjects thoroughly disliked, even when the king anglified them by making them Duchess of Kendal and the Countess of Darlington. One Grub Street rhymer wrote this :

> Come Darlington and Kendal now arise,
> And open wide your lustful bovine eyes.
> The King has said to our profound relief,
> "My German harlots now are English beef."

George as it happened had a poor opinion not only of English beef but of almost everything in the country of his adoption. No English cook could dress a dinner, no English cook could select a dessert. No English coachman could drive nor any English jockey ride a horse. And these were only the beginning of his complaints. He told patient courtiers that they didn't know how to enter a room. The men could talk only about politics and the women spoke only of their ugly clothes. In Hanover all was perfection. Men were paragons of politeness and gallantry. All the women were beautiful, witty and entertaining. In spite of all this, the king decided to take an English mistress, a raven-haired beauty who had learnt her trade at the Stock Exchange. He kept this poor girl so short of cash that she was constantly in debt and had to rely for pocket money on his two valets, Mustapha and Mahomet. He had brought these young men from Turkey because of their intimate knowledge about how to conduct a harem.

After some time at court, the English miss decided that life was better around Cornhill, where a girl good at her job could make fifty pounds a week. She must have found life much happier there than being in the unenvious position of tolerating the baleful glares of the two German harlots and sharing her favours between her royal master and the two lusty young Turks. Everybody who knew him agreed that this first of the Hanoverians was a blockhead, completely without discretion or good taste.

His inability to choose the right people for friends in England was evident when he invited to court the infamous Lady Macclesfield, who was without either virtue or shame. She was of her period the best example of a female rake. When she set her eye on a man she desired she would stop at nothing to get him. Soon after she became a widow she was looking through her window when she saw a strikingly handsome man about to be arrested by bailiffs for debt. Being without a satisfactory lover just then she went out to the street, paid whatever money the bailiff's men demanded and invited the gentleman inside. His name was Brett, a colonel, who always lived beyond his means. He was the lover of the Countess for years and eventually she decided to marry him. Their daughter, Anne Brett, grew up to be one of the most attractive young women in London. She was even more highly sexed than her mother had been. When it was arranged that she should join the royal harem she ruled the court with an iron hand. If the duties of Mustapha and Mahomet had been to find women for the king—part of their job now was to look out for young men who would meet with the demands of Mistress Brett.

When George I died in 1727, his son succeeded to the throne. He also had a German mistress, Madame Malmoden, who had been the belle of all the married women in Hanover. George brought her to London and made her Countess of Yarmouth. With delightful candour he wrote to the queen, "You must love Sophia Malmoden and she will love you."

Sophia was plump and luscious. Shortly before her importation from Germany, the king wrote to his queen, Caroline, sixty pages of a letter, praising in detail all the desirable physical qualities of his new mistress. This second George, as Landor wrote, was undoubtedly "worser" than the first. The German mistress was soon out of favour. George was not so forgiving as Charles II when he found one of his young Hanoverian lieutenants coming out of Sophia's bedroom window. He sent the culprit back to Germany, discarded the Countess and took a new English mistress, Anne Howard, "one of the vainest and prettiest women who ever lived."

This second George was a small dapper man. He spent each evening playing cards with one or other of his mistresses, he ate a huge supper at 11 o'clock and was always in bed by midnight. Because of his habit of making faces even on the most solemn occasion, a fellow European monarch called him "the comedian." He was exceptionally mean about money. When he set up the Countess of Suffolk as still another mistress in St. James's Palace, he made her a miserly allowance and gave her husband an annuity of only £1,200. Most of the ladies at his court found him disgusting. His Germanic sense of humour was lavatorial. Appropriately enough, he died on a water closet newly installed in St. James Palace. One versifier wrote an obituary :

At night he drank a dozen tots.
By day he took his posset.
His life began with chamber pots
And ended on a closet.

A radical change took place at court when "Farmer"
George II became king in 1760. He took as his queen Princess Charlotte of Mecklenburgh-Strelitz, by no means a
beauty but one who liked a quiet domestic life. She was not
popular with the ladies of her court. As she grew older
one of them said about her, "I think the bloom of her
ugliness is fading."

When there was little diversion for them at the palace,
the courtiers had to find other outlets for their energies.
The third George had the longest of the Hanoverian reigns.
His sixty years on the throne brought clubs to their highest
pitch. There were drinking and gambling clubs for the
wealthy and ale meeting places for the ordinary citizen.
This was also the day of the salon, where the lewd and
aristocratic ladies held courts of their own. Their husbands
had their mistresses, the ladies had their lovers. In earlier
times, the bawdy houses had been mostly filthy and insani-
tary hovels. The better class brothels now blossomed out
in a grand manner, in large houses sumptuously furnished
and perfumed beds for the customers.

The more elegant courtesans set up their own establishments in good districts, kept servants and a coach. If business was declining, they would not deign to ply for hire in
the streets. They were to be found at the fashionable hairdressers, sitting at windows where they could easily be seen.
If they walked at all and had an encouraging glance from
a beau, a handkerchief was discreetly dropped.

They would saunter gracefully through St. James's Park
or drive along slowly in an open coach. If a young stranger
smiled, the coachman knew to slacken his speed, so that
the prospective customer could follow to the house. Business
was also done through paid pimps, most of them young and
impoverished men of breeding who dressed and spoke as
well as the visitors with whom they struck up acquaintance
in the hotels or select coffee houses. But lovemaking was
not only the prerogative of the professional ladies. The

maids of honour at court were no more virtuous than they had ever been. The difference was that under George III and Queen Caroline they had not so much license. A Miss Vane, nevertheless, who had borne a child to the Prince of Wales and had become a prude in her later years, was shocked at the nocturnal fun and games that went on in Kensington Gardens, where, she reported to the queen, some of her maids, especially Lady Betty Nightingale, spent the entire summer nights in the arbours with young men.

There were few servants in this royal household. "Farmer" George liked to supervise the agricultural work going on at his country estates. He rose early each morning and made breakfast for himself and the queen. A contemporary cartoon showed him toasting muffins, with Her Majesty admonishing her daughters not to take too much sugar and "save Papa expense."

George II, who had made only one lapse from the straight and narrow path with a young lady in waiting, knew about the increase of vice in London. One of his first acts as king was to issue a proclamation against immorality. It had exactly the opposite effect from what was intended. Whoremongering and rakery were reaching new dimensions. In 1750, during the first decade of this reign, Sir Francis Dashwood founded the Hell-Fire Club at West Wycombe. The members celebrated the black mass, called themselves "monks" and brought from London prostitutes to take part in the orgies dressed as "nuns." The strangest member of the order was the Chevalier D'Eon de Beaumont, whose sex for many years remained in doubt. One, indeed, might have addressed him, as Charles Lamb did in a letter to a Mr. Bensusan—"Dear Sir—or Madam." The "monks" included the Prime Minister of England, the Lord Mayor of London and a few earls. But this is a story which must be told later.

The Prince of Wales, who was on terms of intimate friendship with most of the "monks", was believed to be an honorary member and always a welcome guest. This may or may not be true. It certainly was not commonly known nor—if it was the case—as much publicised as other activities of the Prince. "Farmer" George had always some family scandal on his hands. His brother, Henry, Duke of Cumberland, was but one thorn in the royal flesh. His status is high among the Georgian rakes.

Henry, "a gay little man who hated the clergy," was the life and soul of any party in the exclusive brothels. He had a passion for women as great as his love of gambling. While he made his nightly rounds of the gaming houses and bordellos, his Duchess, a beautiful and witty woman, had her salon at their house in Pall Mall. Her language was so foul that her servants said they had to wash their ears after listening to her. Some nights the Duke would come home early. Then to pass the time he would preside over a faro bank on the street outside his home and could be heard shouting loudly, "Don't punt more than ten guineas—and no tick." All went well enough with this merry way of spending the time till Henry got himself entangled with Lady Grosvenor. Her husband was not so easily placated as other cuckolds; the king had to pay him £10,000 to keep the affair out of court.

Worse still was the fact that his favourite son, the Duke of York, took a mistress, Mary Ann Clarke, a handsome lass who came from Ball and Pin Alley near Chancery Lane and had passed many men through her hands. The Duke set her up in a mansion at Gloucester Place. She kept there twenty servants, among them three male cooks, three coachmen and ten horses. She had been both a prostitute and a small-time actress. Most of the girls who frequented her house belonged to both these callings. Young men with money were always welcome visitors.

Mary Ann was always short of cash. Many of the rich young men she knew were junior army officers and dearly wanted promotion. Mary Ann willingly accepted money from them and persuaded her lover who was Commander in Chief of the Army to show them preference. This was clearly a matter that could not long go unnoticed. The word went round that if a lieutenant wanted to become a captain or a major, all he had to do was consult Mary Ann Clark. It was left to an army colonel to bring the easily obtainable evidence before the authorities. Mary Ann was called before the Bar of the House of Commons and publicly disgraced.

But she was a clever girl, this Mary Ann. She sold the bawdy letters the Duke had written to her for £7,000. They are now, I believe, in the possession of an American collector of famous love-letters. These were but a few of the problems of George III. It is little wonder that he was soon to go mad.

An unusual event in his life happened one night in May, 1800, when signs of his approaching insanity began to appear. He and Queen Charlotte were attending Drury Lane Theatre to see a play he had commissioned called *She Would and She Wouldn't*. As they entered the royal box the orchestra struck up the National Anthem, a man rose from the stalls and fired a shot at the royal party, which included the Duke of York, now forgiven for his misdemeanours. Nobody was wounded and the man, James Hadfield, was immediately arrested.

There were all the indications of another royal scandal when Hadfield appeared in court and it became known that the Duke of York was to give evidence. The first witness was Joseph Holroyd, who told the judge that he had been sitting beside the prisoner in the theatre and had restrained him after the shot was fired. William Wakelin, a hairdresser, said that he had sold Hadfield a pair of pistols for eight shillings. John Truelove, a cobbler, had been drinking with the prisoner on the night of the shooting at Mrs. Mahon's tavern near Drury Lane. There was a tense moment when the Clerk of the Court called "His Royal Highness, the Duke of York." As the Duke stepped into the box, Hadfield stood up and shouted, "I know you well—and you know me."

And that was true. Hadfield had been the Duke's orderly during the wars in Belgium and France. His reason for firing the shot was that he believed the end of the world was about to come at any moment and that England was in no state to face the day of judgment. The judge accepted this as a fair enough explanation and sentenced Hadfield to life imprisonment in Bedlam.

The worries of kingdom were beginning to show on George III. He had no regard for his heir-apparent and young George, the future Prince Regent and king, had no love for his father, if only for the strong parental control exercised in his early manhood. Toasted muffins and no women were not to the taste of the young man who was to become the greatest of these royal rakes.

The king to be was a stripling when he began to make passes at Mary Hamilton, six years his senior and companion to his sisters. There was evidence of his conceit and vanity when he declared his love for her in a letter and described himself :

> I am now approaching the bloom of youth. I am rather above the average size, my limbs well proportioned and on the whole well made, tho' rather too great a penchant to grow fat. My features are strong and manly, a good mouth, tho' rather large, with fine teeth, a tolerable good chin. My sentiments and thoughts are open and generous. I am rather too fond of women and wine.

The prince's infatuation for Mary Hamilton didn't last long. He was seventeen when he fell in love with the beautiful Mrs. Robinson, whom he had seen in the part of Perdita in *A Winter's Tale*. Mrs. Fitzherbert, with whom he went through a marriage ceremony, Lady Conyngham, the beautiful Lady Hertford and many other mistresses were to follow. But the story of the Prince Regent's love affairs has been often told. Among his boon companions were Beau Brummell, the playwright, Richard Brinsley Sheridan, many actors and the three dissolute Barrymore brothers, who were known as Hellgate, Oldgate and Cripplegate. Their sister who had a foul tongue was called Billingsgate.

It had become clear that George III was mad. He suffered from delusions, he rambled incessantly, on one occasion for sixteen hours. He caught his heir by the throat and rammed him against a wall. A bill was passed through Parliament and in February, 1811, the future George IV was appointed Regent.

Those were the days when the Regency bucks and rakes had their wildest fling. The Prince was then in his fiftieth year and so gross in appearance that he was greeted with derision when he entertained Louis of France in London after the fall of Napoleon. Louis was so fat that his legs could scarcely support his enormous paunch and body. Arm in arm, he and the Prince Regent staggered into the hotel where the reception was held at Albemarle Street.

> And France's hope and Britain's heir,
> Were truth a most congenial pair,
> Two round tunbellied thriving rakes,
> Like oxen fed on linseed cakes.

Even that most gentle of men, Charles Lamb, who had called George "The Prince of Whales" couldn't resist the temptation to add to the general ridicule.

> Not a fatter fish than he
> Flounders round the Polar sea.
> See his blubbers and his gills.
> What a lot of drink he swills!

The Regency days were prosperous for many. With more money in his pocket the clerk and the artisan could afford some luxuries denied in earlier times. The women of the less exalted brothels dressed better and demanded better treatment. The English were more addicted than ever before to their three sources of pleasure—women, wine and food. Never before perhaps in any function in London had more food and wine been consumed than at the feast which followed the coronation of George IV. On the tables were:

160 tureens of soup, turtle, rice and vermicelli; 160 dishes of fish, turbot, trout and salmon: 160 hot joints, venison, beef, mutton and veal: 160 dishes of vegetables, potatoes, peas and cauliflowers; 480 sauce boats.

The list is interminable. There were hundreds of dishes of braised ham, fowl and shellfish, with gallons of wine and spirits to wash them down. The peeresses in the gallery who had not eaten since early morning sat watching their menfolk gorging themselves, until some of the lords brought legs of chickens and other delicacies. The noble ladies of England, more aware than ever that fingers were made before knives or forks, went into a free for all scramble.

The most notable absentee was the queen from whom George had long parted. As he drove to the coronation ceremony, people shouted at him, "Hi, Georgie, where's your wife?" The queen had driven herself from her home in Piccadilly in an open carriage and had demanded entrance by knocking on the Abbey door. She swore at the attendants who said that she could not be allowed to enter without a ticket. She drove back home jeered at by the riff-raff making merry in the streets.

The king withdrew early from the festivities. It had been a national holiday. The taverns and the brothels were doing a roaring trade. Not since Charles II had there been a more rakish or lecherous monarch than George IV. Now his days of philandering were over. For some time past he had been taking heavy doses of laudanum to ease the pains in his bladder.

He was living now in the past; in these declining years he had kind thoughts about the roistering friends of his early days. He wrote to one of his ministers :

> An impulse induces me to desire you to enquire into the distressed circumstances of the poor old Irish actor O'Keefe, now ninety years of age and stone blind, whom I knew formerly, having met him at parties of my juvenile recreation and hilarity.

He could take pleasure now only at second hand. He liked to hear about scandal and to read reports of dirty linen being washed in court. He must have enjoyed, as many Londoners did, the scandal about "Little Breeches" and one of his favourite actors.

5

THE THEATRE RAKES

Never meddle with actors, for they are a favoured class.

When Cervantes expressed that opinion he was not being as eccentric as his own Don Quixote nor tilting at a windmill theatre. He knew that from the earliest times successful actors had been pampered by adoring women. In the Victorian era, the admirers of Lewis Waller formed themselves into what must have been the most enthusiastic fan club of all time. Waller was as great an idol of the stage as Valentino was later on the silent screen. Handsome and melodious in voice, Waller was the favourite actor of Edward VII and the friend of Mrs. Langtry, "the Jersey Lily," who married the son of an Irish shipowner and left him to take up the stage as a profession. Her name has always been associated with Edward VII but their story cannot yet be told.

Waller played mostly parts in which the chin-up, clean-limbed Englishman upheld the old flag and the playing fields of Eton against all evil opposition. A coloured man in one play had the audacity to threaten him with a knife. An angry lady member of "The Society of Wallerites" jumped from her seat in the stalls and cried out indignantly, "How dare he?" In much the same way Edmund Kean was worshipped by many women. One of them got him into serious trouble.

When Charlotte Cox watched him from a box in a theatre at Taunton, she fell into a swoon. Thus began the story of "Little Breeches," the most discussed scandal in the final years of the Georgian reign. Most people knew that Kean was a libertine and a rake. He found his women generally in the less reputable pubs and brothels in the London he had known from childhood. He had little regard for the female members of his own profession. This may have begun during his early days as an actor in Ireland. One of his first engagements was with a stock company in Belfast. He flatly refused there to play Romeo with a Juliet eleven years old, Little Miss Mudie, a child prodigy who later was to make a brief appearance at Covent Garden. Kean stamped out of the theatre to "The Bear's Paw," the best brothel in the town, whose proprietress prided herself on keeping nothing but the best drink and the best girls for her clients, who were mainly artists, medical students and young lawyers. The Crown Solicitor of the town was one of her best customers. An angry young man came in one night and asked to see a girl who had overcharged him a crown for her services. "This is a respectable house," said the proprietress. "The young lady you have mentioned is at present engaged upstairs with the Crown Solicitor. If you want a half crown solicitor, you'll not get one here—but there are plenty outside in the streets."

Charlotte Cox was a romantic wanton. One of the people she admired most was Emma Hamilton, who also swooned when she first saw Nelson on his arrival at Naples after the battle of the Nile. Emma cried "Is this possible?" Then she fainted in her hero's arms. Emma, of course, made history. All Lottie Cox did was to put an end to the career of England's greatest tragedian. People had grown tired hearing and reading about royalty and their mistresses. The love affair of a popular actor was better news. Kean was a public figure on both sides of the Atlantic. Lottie was the wife of a London alderman and banker. What more could the gossip writers want?

After her fainting act in the theatre, Mrs. Cox was carried backstage. Kean was so considerate that her husband invited him to dinner. The friendship between Kean and Lottie ripened. She often visited him in his dressing room at the theatre and at the pubs where he stayed in London. The letters read in court showed how ardent the love affair had been. The husband, it seemed, thought nothing of the friendship until he discovered some of Kean's letters in Lottie's boudoir. He immediately sued Kean for criminal conversation. The public interest was aroused when the alderman brandished a pistol at the stage door of the theatre where Kean was appearing and had to be forcibly removed. The pending law case was the talk of the town. The scandal writers sharpened their pencils and trimmed their quill pens.

As was only to be expected the court was crowded when the story of Kean and his "Little Breeches" was heard before Lord Chief Justice Abbott and a special jury. The wives and daughters of the city men as well as the ladies of the streets had queued from early morning to get in. They expected to be entertained by the proceedings and they were not disappointed. There were roars of laughter when extracts from the letter were read. The term "Little Breeches" caught the public fancy. Mrs. Bloomer had not yet arrived to make popular a new name for feminine underwear and women's lingerie were still the unmentionables.

Mrs. Patrick Campbell, even more popular as an actress than Lily Langtry made the newspaper headlines at her first appearance on the London stage when some of her underwear slipped off and she picked it up as casually as if she had merely dropped a handkerchief. Whether or not Mrs. Pat did this for publicity we shall never know. The music hall comedians were quick off the mark to make rhymes about her slip as they did in another song of the period :

Lottie Collins lost her drawers.

Lottie Cox also provided the comedians with material. The derivation of the word "toff" to describe a gentleman has never been clear nor has the term "toffee-nosed," meaning a snob, been traced to its origin. But "toff" was known not only in London but in Ireland in Kean's time. *The Belfast Magpie* reported :

Lottie was a city lady,
Married to a toff,
She put on her little breeches,
An actor took them off.

In one of his letters to Lottie, Kean had written :

On Sunday night I will be back in London. Tonight in my imagination, I will hold my "Little Breeches" in my arms and sleep in spite of thunder.

The jury was in no doubt that misconduct had taken place. The case for the defence was that the alderman had condoned his wife's intimacy with Kean and had often left them alone together. He had claimed £2,000 as damages. The judge awarded him £800.

Never before had such publicity been given to a law case. In a published account of the proceedings, there was a drawing showing Lottie holding up her skirt and revealing a pair of frilled breeches which Kean used in one of his parts. She had put them on while he was on the stage and she was waiting in his dressing room. She is saying to Kean, "Don't you think they fit me well? I'll wear them, unless you want to take them off." And the adoring Kean is replying, "I shall call you 'Little Breeches' from now on." In his book, *Mad Genius*, Willson Disher quotes from a broadsheet :

With his ginger tail he did assail and did the prize obtain,
The merry little wanton Banting Cock of Drury Lane.
She wrote to him a letter and sealed it with a ring,
And bade him come at twelve at night and she would let him in.
So softly she stole down the stairs and did the door unlock.
"My blessings on King Dick," she said, "he is a hearty Cock.
The servant maids are all asleep, my husband is from home.
My chamber is so very dull, I cannot lie alone."
"O, Little Breeches, you're the girl I ever shall adore.
I feel more happy in your arms that e'er I did before."

All his life Edmund Kean had been up to hell-rakery in one shape or another. After his early days in Ireland, he returned to the London he loved. He had been born there, the illegitimate son of an Irish hawker girl, Anne Carey, who made her living selling fruit and occasionally as a "walk-on" actress. As a boy, young Edmund roamed the streets, picking up a few pence here and there, listening to actors talking and resolving that one day he would tread the stage. Before he was fifteen he knew every ale house and brothel within a mile of Covent Garden. He ran errands for the players and got into the gallery free to see the Shakespearean parts which were to make his future reputation. Hazlitt wrote, "To see Kean act is like reading Shakespeare by lightning."

When he became famous, Ned, as he was known to his friends, led the same wayward life he had known in his younger years. Most of his leisure time was spent in the company of street traders, boxers, thieves and their girl friends. He rode his horse, Shylock, through the centre of London at all hours of the night and day. He kept a young lion in his room and hypnotised it with the magic spell he had over his audience in the theatre. He was loved by the ragtag and bobtail of London. That may have been why they turned against him when they learned that he had been hob-nobbing with the wife of an alderman.

On the morning after the court verdict, *The London Times* reported :

> That obscene little personage, Kean, is, we see, to make his reappearance at Drury Lane. His real friends must now desert him when they realise him dead to the lowest degree of shame which distinguishes animal from human behaviour.

After this warning from the most important paper in the land, Kean's friends tried to dissuade him from playing in London until the scandal of "Little Breeches" had been forgotten. They found him in bed with a glass of brandy in his hand being entertained by a dancing girl. In the room also was an acrobat doing somersaults over tables and chairs. Kean was adamant. Had he not been the friend of the Prince Regent who was now king? Was he not the greatest actor in England? The court decision and "Little Breeches" was only a trifle. Confident that his friends would support him, he would appear in his favourite part of Richard III as advertised at Drury Lane.

The theatre was packed to capacity. Before the curtain rose, the audience had become an almost uncontrollable mob. Londoners who had long condoned laxity in royal morals were not prepared to accept such behaviour in their most popular stage idol. As soon as Kean appeared they cried out in derision :

> "Little Breeches. Little Breeches. Tell us about 'Little Breeches.' "

Kean's boxer friends tried to keep order as brawls broke

out in the pit. Prostitutes hurled obscenities at him when he tried to speak.

When he appeared next evening as Othello, the reception was even worse. Those who had acclaimed him in the past and whose morals were no better than his own were determined to drive him from the London stage. Realising that he was no longer wanted in the West End, he sailed to America to fulfil engagements there. The story of "Little Breeches" had been as widely read there as it was in England. He was booed at every performance. The critic of *The New York Advertiser* wrote :

> No theatre manager should allow such a lump of immoral pollution to contaminate his stage. Every female must stay away and males hiss him with indignation.

America, he discovered, was more puritanical than England. He sailed home, a broken man. His last appearance on the London stage was in 1883 when he was forty-four. All that day he had been drinking heavily. As he was about to deliver one of his long speeches as Othello, he fell. The curtain was quickly lowered. He died soon afterwards leaving many memories and debts amounting to more money than he had ever earned.

The tragedy of Edmund Kean is no sadder than that of George Farquhar, who had also begun his stage career in Ireland. In London he became more famous as a playwright than as an actor. Unlike Kean, he preferred the company of women in his own profession. One of his mistresses, Susan Verbruggen, "was fair, plump and full featured with breasts adorned with the most beautiful moles."

Farquhar liked describing the charms of his women friends. Mrs. Verbruggen was an intellectual and a wit. Susan Carroll, less important as an actress, was a more amusing and earthy lass. From both of them, Farquhar got inspiration for his bawdy plays. He spent six hours each day writing and in the company of these two mistresses. He wrote :

> So there's twelve of the twenty-four hours gone. The other twelve I dispose of in two things. In the first four I toast myself drunk. In the other eight, I sleep myself sober again.

When George Farquhar died at the age of twenty-seven, a friend said that his epitaph should be, "He loved too many women, drank too much wine and wrote too few plays."

Few men have packed more into a short span of life than this son of an Irish clergyman. As an undergraduate at Trinity College, Dublin, he went one day to Donnybrook Fair, an event where drinking, gambling and wenching went on for a week. When trouble arose over women, Farquhar drew his sword and seriously wounded a young country-man. With a howling mob in pursuit, he escaped from the fairground with his life. His next piece of sword play was a turning point in his career. He had stopped studying at the university and became an actor. While appearing at Smock Alley Theatre, he and a fellow player had spent the night and early morning in a brothel and had drunk steadily through the day. They staggered to the theatre to get ready for the play. Farquhar had forgotten to put a foil on his sword. He came to this speech :

> Friendship with him whose hand did Osman kill,
> Base as he was, he was my brother still,
> And since his blood has wiped away his guilt,
> Nature asks thine for that which thou has spilt.

Farquhar lurched forward and stabbed his friend in the chest.

The young player, Digby Price, lay at death's door for several days. Farquhar swore that he would never draw a sword and never act again. He never did. With forty pounds in his pocket, he set out for London with the intention of becoming an author. He haunted the taverns of the city. At the Mitre in Fleet Street, he first saw the girl who was to become the greatest influence on his life.

She was a beautiful creature of sixteen, with a shapely figure and large dark eyes. She told him that her name was Anne Oldfield, that she was barmaid at the inn and wanted to become an actress. It was inevitable that she was to become young George Farquhar's first London mistress. It was inevitable also that she was to have many other men. When Farquhar had helped her to realise her ambition, she took as a lover the son of Sir Winston Churchill, father of the Duke of Marlborough, and bore him a son. She found an even wealthier protector in Sir Arthur Mainwaring, M.P. for Preston, and had two illegitimate children by him. When he died, Miss Oldfield inherited all his money. She was a rich woman when Farquhar lay dying in poverty. But Anne Oldfield had always been the one woman he loved and he never quite forgave her unfaithfulness.

It was all but impossible for an actress to resist temptation in those days. The wealthy young bucks of the town were always hot in pursuit. It was not uncommon for one of them to jump on to the stage and mingle with the players. One young man climbed over the orchestra pit to follow to her dressing room George Anne Bellamy and make passionate passes at her. Miss Bellamy would not have objected if the time and place had been better chosen. Another young rake mounted the stage and put his hand into Peg Woffington's bosom when she was appearing as Cordelia and the head of her ancient father, King Lear, was resting on her lap. Miss Woffington, "the most cuddled and caressed" of all women, sought after by wealthy rakes, gently removed the young man's hand and went on with the show.

Peg Woffington was the most enchanting of all female rakes since the days of Nell Gwynn. For her success as an actress, she owed everything to George Farquhar. Her first appearances on the London stage were in male parts in his plays. She was what you might call the first of "the principal boys." In Farquhar's comedy, *The Recruiting Officer*, she was a riot as a girl who joins the army in men's clothes. She was even more successful as Sir Harry Wildair in another of Farquhar's plays, *The Constant Couple*. She played this part hundreds of times and her admirers always demanded more. After an ovation one evening, she said to one of the actors in the green room, "Half the rakes of London must believe me to be a man." He assured her that the other half of the town had intimate knowledge of the fact that she was a woman.

Peg was completely promiscuous. Immediately after her death in 1760, Samuel Bladon published a pamphlet, *The*

Memoirs of the Celebrated Mrs. Woffington, with the sub-title, "The Amours of Many Persons of Rank." His stories about her numerous affairs may be slightly exaggerated. She was, however, never ashamed to admit that she had more lovers than most actresses, some of them, like David Garrick, in her own profession, most of them men of high rank. She was fifteen when she took her first lover in Dublin. Like Nell Gwynn, she had sold fruit outside the theatres. As a child she had been carried across a tight-rope each evening by Madame Violante. Like Fanny Hill and so many others, Peg had no alternative but to sell her favours. As can be seen from her portraits by Reynolds, Hogarth and other artists, she was a beautiful creature. Her first serious attachment was with the son of an Irish squire. He brought her to London and deserted her.

She had known quite a lot about vice in the Irish capital. She was to learn much more about life now on a grander scale. George II was on the throne. While he was enjoying himself with his bevy of mistresses, the royal dukes and noblemen found their entertainment around the theatres and the coffee houses and taverns. In the summer evenings, decorated barges full of young men and women sailed down the Thames to Vauxhall Gardens to make merry on the green swards under the shade of great trees. Madame Violante had also arrived in the big city. This advertisement appeared in the *Daily Post* :

> At the Particular Desire of Several Persons of Quality for the Benefit of the famous Signora Violante, who has just arrived with a new extraordinary fine Company. At the new Theatre in Haymarket will be presented the most surprising performances that ever were shown in the English theatre—To which is added The Beggar's Opera after the Irish manner, which was performed 96 times in Dublin with great Applause—the part of Macheath by the celebrated Miss Woffington.

It is not surprising that a girl so vivacious and beautiful as Peg found admirers among young men of rank. The memoirs of her life is a catalogue of one affair after another, with a duke, a lord, a gambling peer and a colonel. Her best biographer, Janet Camden Lucey, wrote :

Peg is made to outshine all the leading courtesans of the century. Fanny Murray, Lucy Cooper and Kitty Fisher appear as angels by comparison.

Her stage success in London really began when she called to see the pantomime king, John Rich, at his home in Bloomsbury. She found him there drinking tea and nibbling toast, surrounded by his twenty-seven cats. He offered her an immediate engagement. She was twenty-four when she appeared at Covent Garden before the Prince of Wales and a distinguished audience in *The Recruiting Officer*. Rhymes by the dozen were written about her :

> The beautiful Peg who showed such a leg,
> When lately she dressed in men's clothes.
> A creature uncommon who's both man and woman,
> The chief of the belles and the beaux.

The playbill for this occasion read as follows :

COVENT GARDEN.
By Command of His Royal Highness, the Prince of Wales.
BY THE COMPANY OF COMEDIANS.
This evening at six will be presented.
THE RECRUITING OFFICER.
Written by the Late Mr. Farquhar.
The Part of Sylvia by Miss Woffington.
(being the first time of her performing on this stage.)

It was by no means the last time that the flower-seller girl from Dublin was to appear at Covent Garden. The royal box that evening was festooned with a canopy of silk, richly adorned with scarlet and gold tassels. All the elite of London were there, gay ladies and gentlemen of the court, with their wigs and swords and snuff boxes. The orchestra played an overture, the footlight candles were snuffed and up went the heavy velvet curtain. The hero of the piece was a rakehellery officer, Captain Plume, who boasted that he had been constant to fifteen women at a time and never melancholy for one of them. Peg played Sylvia, "a young gentlewoman with the constitution of a horse." The captain was subdued when she told him :

I am not troubled with spleen, cholic or vapours. I need no salts for my stomach, nor wash for my complexion. I can gallop all morning after the hunting horn and all evening after a fiddle. In fact, I can do anything were I to be put on trial.

This was the stuff to give the troops. The Prince was convulsed with laughter as Peg slapped a shapely thigh and put the captain in his place. The late Mr. Farquahar had made another bright star shine in the London theatre. But Peg had always been as lucky in her authors as she had been in her lovers. If he had not been so fully occupied with so many other fair ladies, she could have had the Prince of Wales—but there were too many ardent young men at her beck and call. Edward Moore expressed her character perfectly when he wrote the part of Rosetta for her in his comedy, *The Foundling*. Her big speech in this play was :

Power! Power! my dear, sleeping or waking, is a charming thing. The men will come when we call 'em and go when we send 'em. They are like other beasts of prey. You must tame 'em by hunger, but if once you feed 'em high, they are apt to run wild and forget their keepers.

With tailor-made lines like this to fit her, Peg was the toast of London and the envy of all her rival actresses. As she travelled by sedan chair or coach to the theatre people would nudge each other and say, "There's Peg Woffington." She loved men and was never except by her own desire without a sleeping partner. In Bow Street she set up house with two actors, "Wicked" Charlie Macklin and David Garrick. This was a bohemian menage.

"Wicked" Charlie was a fighting Irishman, as tempestuous as David Garrick was timid. Charlie's career began when he robbed his mother and ran off to London to take his first job as a pot-boy in a pub.

He graduated from there to take over White's gaming club. When he had lost all his money there he found another backer to finance a pub venture at Covent Garden. At last he realised his ambition to become an actor. At a time when the rebellion in Scotland had made that country and its people unpopular in England, he insisted on playing Macbeth in a kilt. When he made his name in *The Merchant of Venice*, Pope, who was not easily pleased, wrote :

This is the Jew that Shakespeare knew.

George II, "the comedian king," was having trouble then with his House of Commons, mainly because they thought he was spending too much money on his German mistresses. "Tell them," he told his Prime Minister, Sir Robert Walpole, "to go and see that Irishman playing Shylock at Covent Garden."

"Wicked" Charlie was seldom out of trouble. After a squabble over a wig in the green room at Covent Garden, he killed a fellow actor with a karate blow. He was tried for murder and found not guilty. "His language," somebody said, "would make any harlot blush, nor was he to be softened into modesty by sex, beauty or age." This was the man with whom Peg chose to keep house at Bow Street. She always acknowledged that Garrick was her lover but she admitted that she could never be faithful to any one man. She discarded her admirers as calmly as a gambler would the worthless losers in a hand of cards. She was with Macklin and Garrick one evening in Bow Street when the young Earl of Darnley knocked loudly on the door.

The wig which Garrick in his haste to leave her bedroom dropped in the corridor was picked up by Darnley who accused Peg of having had another lover in. She was ready with an answer. The wig was one she intended to wear for her next part as a male impersonator. Darnley was satisfied with this explanation and Peg and he spent the night happily together. An endearing thing about Peg Woffington was her complete honesty about her love affairs. Admirers in the pit would often call out good-naturedly, "Who did you sleep with last night, Peg?" And she would stop in the middle of a speech and tell them. If it wasn't the Earl of Darnley it was the Duke of Rutland or some other nobleman. She dallied for a few years with Sir Charles Hanbury Williams, M.P. for Monmouth and Paymaster-General for the Royal Marines. There was always in the background a colonel in the Guards, a descendant of Sir Julius Caeser, who had been Clerk of the Exchequer during the reign of James I. She was the girl who just could not say "No." "Forgive her one female weakness," wrote Arthur Murphy, another of her lovers, "and she is adorned with every other virtue."

Practically nothing is known about Peg's father, apart from some evidence that he was a Dublin bricklayer. We know that she kept her mother well supplied with money and that she was generous in every way. When her Irish maid was getting married, she gave her a hundred guineas. She did even better for her sister, Polly, an unsuccessful actress who became one of the most important women in England.

She married pretty Polly off to a handsome young officer, son of the Earl of Cholmondeley, the Lord Lieutenant of Wales, who was in debt up to his armpits. When he heard that his favourite son, Robert, had married "a player's sister," he went to see Peg. He was so overcome by her charm that he gave his approval to the marriage and was honest enough to admit that his estate was mortgaged and that neither he nor his son had a ha'penny to scratch themselves with. Peg's reply was typical. She told the earl that she had been maintaining poor relations and beggars most of her life and that another one in the family—especially with a name like Cholmondeley—wouldn't matter one way or the other. Soon after the marriage, young Robert Cholmondeley left the army and took a safer job as a clergyman. He finished up as Vicar of Hertford.

Polly Woffington was much more fortunate than some of the theatre people of her day. A few of them married into the aristocracy, more died young and in poverty like George Anne Bellamy. Anne Bracegirdle, the daughter of Justinian Bracegirdle of Northampton, lived to be eighty-five. Macaulay called her "a cold, vain coquette, who would flirt with any admirer in the knowledge that no flame she might kindle would thaw her own ice."

Peg Woffington was forty when she died, comforted to the end by the faithful Colonel Caeser. Forsaken by all her other noble lovers, she had returned to him. "She had," as somebody said, "rendered at last unto Caesar the things that were Caesars." In all the references to this long love affair, the christian name of "The Colonel" is never mentioned. Peg was his Cleopatra. Maybe, like his ancestor, his christian name was Julius. Wanton, strumpet, courtesan, amoral sexually—call her what you like—Peg Woffington

had been more honoured than any other actress on the
British stage. At least fifty drawings, portraits and busts of
her are to be seen in the National Gallery, the British
Museum, the Victoria and Albert, at Windsor Castle, the
Garrick Club and in private collections.

"The history of the world," wrote Carlyle, "is but the
biography of great men." It could be said with equal truth
that the history of the stage begins and ends with the lives
of men and women who were bawds and rakes. Some of
them were buried in Westminster Abbey. There is a memorial to Peg Woffington in Teddington Parish Church, not
far from the home of one man who had never a good word
to say about her.

Young Robert Cholmondeley, Polly Woffington's husband, was a nephew of Horace Walpole, later the Earl of
Orford. If Horace himself was not a womaniser, he made
it his business to find out a lot about the private lives of
those who were. Although Lady Townshend had said that
the only thing Horace ever wanted to kiss was a stuffed
tiger, there were rumours that he had a mild affair with
Kitty Clive, Peg Woffington's only rival as a comedy actress.
We find the name of Horace among those who visited the
Hell-fire club at West Wycombe. It is pretty certain that
he didn't go there to take part in the sexual orgies with the
"monks" and the "nuns" from the London brothels but to
make notes about the goings-on. If Horace had not the
salacious pen of Pepys, he took as much delight as Samuel
did in recording gossip. "Dashwood," he wrote about the
founder of the Hell-Fire Club, "has the staying power of
a stallion and the impetuosity of a bull." How Horace knew
this—unless he was told so by one of the "nuns"—is as
much a matter of speculation as if we were to enquire what
songs the sirens sang to Ulysses and his men. Horace and
other chroniclers of the vices of his period pursued their
jobs assiduously. "Lord S— is the lover of Lucy Cooper,
who is lewder than all the whores of the reign of Charles
II." "There is in vogue a Mrs. Woffington, a bad actress
and an impudent-faced Irish girl. She is on the tapis again
with Lord Darnley." Comments like these are typical of all
the gossip writing of the eighteenth century.

Walpole had no love for Peg Woffington, possibly because he was a snob and she had arranged the marriage between her sister and his nephew. "My nephew," he wrote sadly, "has married a player's sister." Peg Woffington died when she was forty. Polly was married to young Cholmondeley when she was seventeen and lived to be eighty-four, a dear old lady accepted by all the intellectuals. Dr. Johnson held her hand so long on one occasion that "she wondered if he was ever going to give it back to her." Even Walpole came to like her and invited her to go with him on a trip to France.

The Gothic castle which Horace Walpole built and which still stands at Strawberry Hill near Twickenham was a potting shed for gossip. Writers and actors were regular guests. Horace made Kitty Clive the gift of a cottage nearby. David Garrick had a villa half a mile away. A constant visitor was Lady Mary Wortley Montagu, a versatile woman who sometimes acted as a stand-in for one of the harlot "nuns" at West Wycombe. So did a friend of hers, Lady Betty Germain, whose name appears often among the lists of amateur prostitutes. In spite of her status as an actress and her reputation for unchastity, Peg Woffington was never invited to Walpole's castle.

There has always been some doubt about the parentage of Horace Walpole. Officially he was the son of Sir Robert Walpole, one of the greatest of all British prime ministers. It was publicly known that Sir Robert spent his weekends at Richmond with the lovely blonde daughter of a London merchant, Maria Skeritt, and that they had three illegitimate children. Lady Walpole, a flighty girl herself, knew all about this liaison and found lovers in plenty. There is evidence to show that Horace was not the son of Sir Robert, but of Lord Hervey, the eldest son of the Earl of Bristol.

All the Herveys were not only libertines but men of wit and charm. The fourth Earl of Bristol, Frederick Augustus Hervey, Doctor of Divinity, became the Bishop of Derry. He was as fond of lovely women as any man who ever got himself ordained in holy orders. Near his palace at Down-hill in Ireland, he built a temple to one of his mistresses.

There were many rooms in this palace and many ladies

came to stay there. To make sure that they would be his private property, the Bishop, it is said, had flour spread outside their bedrooms in case any of his guests or curates would leave footprints if they wished to go visiting the girls at night. He travelled so often on the Continent with fair ladies that his name is commemorated in the Hotel Bristol you still find in so many European capitals. He was a handsome man this Bishop, with an income of £20,000 a year. He drove in an open coach drawn by six horses. He was dressed usually in purple, with diamond-studded buckles on his shoes and white gauntlet gloves fringed with gold lace. He had excellent taste in the choice of women and works of art. In some respects, Horace Walpole had inherited the best qualities of the Hervey family, including much of their eccentricity.

At Strawberry Hill, Horace set up a private printing press, not to issue bawdy pamphlets such as were appearing daily in London but to make editions of the works of his friend, the poet Thomas Gray, who had been at school with him at Eton. A printer was required. Kitty Clive's rakish brother, George Raftor, who lived with her, was a small-time actor who seldom got work. He brought from London a young actor called Robinson, who had flashing eyes and floating hair which were greatly admired by the homosexual members of his profession. Whatever his gifts were as an actor, Robinson knew little or nothing about the printing trade. Nor did he wish to know anything about the hard drinking amorous ladies to be found round Strawberry Hill. He was much more interested in Horace and would doubtless if given the opportunity have wished to take the place of the stuffed tiger in his master's affection. He wrote to a friend :

I write from this shady bower, nodding groves and amaranthine shades, close by old Father Thames' silver side—Fair Twickenham. In my last letter I informed you that I was going into the country to transact business with a private gentleman, son to the late great Sir Robert Walpole. He is a bachelor and spends his time in the studious rural taste.

Robinson left the letter in a drawer where Horace was

Within the engraving:

LIBERTY

NORTH BRITON
NUMBER 45

NORTH BRITON
NUMBER

John Wilkes Esq.ʳ

Drawn from the Life and Etch'd in Aquafortis by W.ᵐ Hogarth.

Price 1 Shilling.

Publish'd according to Act of Parliament May ᵗ 16. 1763.

Plate 4 JOHN WILKES, defender of liberty and lover of many women. Expelled from the House of Commons for writing the obscene "Essays on Women".

Plate 6
BILLINGSGATE
TRIUMPHANT. A
Dandy comes off second
best in this encounter
with a Billingsgate
virago. The popularity
of Wilkes was such that
cordials were named
after him.

Plate 5 Black Mass rites
in the sanctum at
Medmenham Abbey.
SIR FRANCIS DASH-
WOOD, LORD LE
DESPENCER, assisted
by PAUL WHITE-
HEAD, secretary of the
Hell-Fire Club.

The SECRETS of the CONVENT.

OTENPORA
OMORES

Once on a Time, as Fame reported,
When Friar Paul St. Frances Courted,
Thus Frances answer'd, your no Novice,
You well deserve the Jewel-Office.
A Place of Trust your Faith will suit.
You shall demand it of Laird Boot.
Your MAUVEEN; Morals Virtue, Grace
Call loudly for a goodly Place.
Success attend you, I'll be blunt
My dearest Brother here is ——

bound to find it. Like Queen Victoria on another occasion, Horace was not greatly amused. For some unknown reason, Robinson's days at Strawberry Hill were few. Not for him the task of setting up

> The curfew tolls the bell of parting day.

Or Gray's ode on the sad death of Horace's favourite cat who was drowned in a tub trying to catch goldfish :

> Not all that tempts your wandering eyes
> And heedless hearts is lawful prize,
> Nor all that glisters gold.

Robinson silently stole away from fair Twickenham which, as cruel Lady Townsend said, "would have been a pleasant cool place" if Kitty Clive's brandy face had "not lit it up like a fiery sun." How Peg Woffington would have enjoyed that remark about her rival. The women of those days were much more savage than the males.

Horace, who recorded fully the going and coming of Robinson, continued to churn out his eternal gossip. As a change from writing about the amours of his friends, he looked now and then at the political scene. One afternoon at Westminster, he observed a handsome young man who had written some comedies and was now an M.P. Horace thought that the House of Commons was "no place for the son of an Irish player." The young man whose father had been an actor was Richard Brinsley Sheridan, an ardent lover and a wit.

It was believed that Thomas Sheridan, the father of Richard Brinsley, was one of Peg Woffington's many lovers. They had been seen going off in a coach one night for some unknown destination. The explanation given was that Thomas was not taking Peg away for a night's diversion but to satisfy the stipulation of another of her admirers that he would leave her all his money if she renounced the Catholic faith and became a Protestant. The necessary journey of Thomas Sheridan and Peg, it seems, was to have this conversion made by a clergyman in some remote part of the country. It was as good an excuse as any. It was, moreover, endorsed by the fact that Peg did become an Anglican

3—THR

and inherited thus the basis of her fortune. But whatever kind of gay spark Thomas Sheridan may have been, there can be no question about the love affairs of his famous son. He was the bosom friend of the greatest rake of the period, the Prince Regent.

One evening at Brookes' Club, the Prince, who knew a lot about ample bosoms, put forward the theory to Brinsley that "the reason for a beautiful woman's breasts being the objects of such exquisite delight to men arises from their first pleasureable sensations of warmth and sustenance from infancy." Brinsley considered this proposal for a few seconds, before saying, "I was born with a wooden and not a silver spoon in my mouth. I have had sensual desires aroused by the observation of women's breasts—but never by a wooden spoon."

As a young man, Richard Brinsley Sheridan eloped with and married the beautiful Miss Linley of Bath. He was as unfaithful to her as most of his friends were to their wives. But for the grace of God, he would have been like Kean the principal actor in a law case when he fell in love with the Countess of Bessborough. The husband was reluctantly persuaded to forgive his wife, one of the most beautiful of all Georgian women, an enchantress who could hold the attention of any company in conversation. In her ageing years, Byron irreverently called her "Old Lady Blarney."

When Mrs. Sheridan was equally forgiving and Richard had promised to be a good boy, he was found some hours later locked in her room with the family governess. There was, he explained, no reason for having bolted the door apart from the fact that he wanted to be alone with the young woman without interruption as a painter would be with his model. How else could he put her into one of his plays?

If women were a weakness with Sheridan, gambling and wine were even more paramount. He seldom made a wager for less than £200. He drank heavily every day and in the early mornings. He was not a sipper of strong liquor but, like so many Irishmen, a "knocker back." Give him a glass of whisky in his hand and it went down his throat in a second. When Drury Lane, of which he was lessee at the time, was being destroyed by flames, he sat calmly lowering a bottle in a coffee house nearby. When his friends expressed surprise at his composure, he said, "Surely a man may have a drink at his own fireside."

"Sherry," as his friends called him, was the most likeable and brilliant of all his theatrical contemporaries. Great men asked his advice about the choice of mistresses and how to deal with them. The royal dukes sought his company at every possible moment. Even Lady Bessborough, whom he had treated badly, was at his deathbed. All his money had been lost in speculation in the theatre and in gambling. The bailiffs were downstairs ready to wrap him up in a blanket and carry him off to be imprisoned for debt. The room had so little furniture that Lady Bessborough had to sit on an old trunk as she held his hand. He asked her how he looked and she told him that his eyes were as bright as ever. A few days later, the author of *The School for Scandal* and so many other imperishable comedies, died and was buried in Westminster Abbey.

6

TIPPLING AND BAWDY TALK

These things, according to the gospel of Ned Ward, were the chief concerns of the Londoners he knew. And he made it his business to know a great many of them. When it comes to getting a first-hand account of the lower strata of life of the city during the eighteenth century, he is the best authority. He has always been a neglected writer. Today his name is known only to scholars. His numerous works have never been reprinted, possibly because they are too bawdy. He was a poet, a publican and a pamphleteer, a man of the people. He had little interest in what went on in royal circles. Not a king nor a queen nor a court mistress is mentioned anywhere in his writings. Nor did he care what duke or lord was currently sleeping with this or that famous actress. He was much more interested in the men and women who found their recreations in the common ale houses and the brothels. Occasionally in his paper, *The London Spy*, which was not unlike *The Private Eye* of today, he would look at the ladies and their beaux who strolled in St. James's Park. He observed what went on in the way of sex at the London Stock Exchange and how the wives and daughters attending church services at Covent Garden were more interested in finding there a lover than in their devotions. He knew little or nothing about the high-class courtesans. He preferred to write about Bess Grundy, Moll Bunch or Nan Topley of Clare Market and Billingsgate.

These women had tongues that would scorch the paint off a door but to the men they liked and loved they were as considerate as Doll Tearsheet was to Falstaff. There was, indeed, something Falstaffian about Ned Ward himself. We can see him enjoying convivial company in the ale houses,

laughing heartily as he listened to good liars, quaffing
many pints of ale and all the time making notes for his
paper. When he got a tavern of his own he was a genial
host, who attracted kindred spirits. "Tippling, gossip and
bawdy talk"—these were the pattern of his day. George
Augustis Sala called him "jovial, brutal, vulgar, graphic
New Ward of Grub Street." And that is as good a description as any. He was not by nature vulgar. All he did was
to record truthfully the talk he heard around him every
day. The ordinary Londoner was as profane and as vituper-
ative then as he is today. Four-letter words were common
usage as they are still. Ned Ward set down exactly what he
heard. At times he may have written with his tongue in
cheek and have been needlessly obscene. Much of *The
London Spy* is unprintable. His account of "The Farters'
Club," which met in a tavern near Fleet Street, is a little
too much for my liking. Yet it is no more distasteful than
the stories of Rabalais or some of the verse of Pope or
Swift. Pope, who had a much higher regard for animals
than he had for human beings could write :

> We country dogs love nobler sport
> And scorn the pranks of dogs at court,
> For naughty Fob, where now you come,
> To fart and piss all round the room.

Swift is at times more obscene than Ward. The great dean
could write the most tender passages to the most beloved of
the three women in his life. Listen to him rhapsodizing
Stelle in the "little language" in which she is MD, meaning,
we suppose, "My Darling" and he is PDFR, on which you
may put any interpretation you like :

> Stay, I will answer some of your letter in bed this morning.
> Let me see, come and appear little letter. "Here I am," says
> he, "and what say you to Stella this morning fresh and fast-
> ing. It will be just three weeks when I have your next letter.
> Dearest MD, love your PDFR who has not had one happy
> day since he left you.

There is no explanation why a pillar of the church like
Swift should have forgotten in his later years all the delicacy
of his earlier feeling for women. He was in love with three

of them, Jane Waring, whom he met when he was a curate in Ireland, Esther Vanhomrigh, who chased him from London to Dublin, and Stella, Esther Johnston. Some say he married her and some say not. Some say that she was his half sister and that their love was incestous. There is a theory that he avoided marriage because he had contracted venereal disease, which could easily happen in those unhygienic days.

> Here lies two poor lovers who had the mishap,
> Though very chaste people, to die of the clap.

When all three of his women friends were dead and Swift was living in Ireland with Sir Arthur and Lady Acheson, he began to hate women. How else could he have written this :

> No more that briar thy tender leg shall rake.
> I spare the thistle for Sir Arthur's sake.
> Sharp are the stones, take thou this rushy mat,
> The hardest bum will bruise with sitting squat.
> They breeches, torn behind, stand gaping wide.
> Thy petticoat shall save thy dear backside.
> Nor need you blush, although you feel it wet.
> I vow 'tis nothing else but sweat.

In his life of Swift, John Middleton Murry says that he jibs at but still quotes these lines of Swift :

> O Strephon, 'ere that fatal day,
> When Chloe stole your heart away,
> Had you but through a cranny spy'd
> On house of ease your future bride,
> In all the postures of her face,
> Which Nature gives in such a case.
> Distortions, groanings, strainings, heavings.
> 'Twere better you had licked her leavings.

"It is so perverse," writes Mr. Murry, so unnatural, so humanly wrong. Yet Swift labours it again and again. Another Strephon, peering into his lady's bedroom, discovers the commode :

> Disgusted Strephon slunk away,
> Repeating in his amorous fits,
> Oh, Celia, Celia, Celia shits.

Ned Ward could not equal Dean Swift when it came to writing about the natural functions of the body. They were born in the same year and were contemporary throughout their lives. Both were fond of women. Swift, who was an authority on that subject, gave this advice to Pope :

> Descend in the name of God to some other amusements as common mortals do. Learn to play at cards, get talking about females.

Nobody talked more about females than Swift. Ward was constantly under attack by his enemies for his interest in sex.

> Ward is a brazened, impudent rake. Silk gowns and petticoats are all alike to him. He plays at women as he does at cards. His whore in Little Britain has been besieging his door with a bastard from last Sunday noon both night and day.

This was the accepted style in which rival journalists of Ned Ward's time described each other. If you didn't like what some other scribe wrote about you, you challenged him to a duel. The wiser course was to let his abuse run off you like water off a duck's back. Ned Ward was not a fighting man. When he arrived in London, he was an inexperienced country lad from Oxfordshire, where he had access to a good library in the home of a friend whose name he never mentions. He has, in fact, very little to say about his early days in the hundreds of books, poems and pamphlets he wrote and published at his own expense. This is how he begins his own story :

> After a tedious confinement in the country, where I slept like Diogenes in a tub or as an owl in a hollow tree, taking as much delight in my books as an alchemist in his bellows : but though taking this delight I tired after several years of the search for knowledge. There was no little vexation to a man of my genius to find my brain loaded to no purpose. This reflection put me in as great a panic as a beau does when he daubs his clothes or makes a false step in an approach to a possible mistress.

You will realise that young Ned Ward had a high opinion of himself and that he would succeed in the city. He had no doubt that he would find there a suitable outlet for his talent. In *The London Spy,* he explained his reason for leaving home.

"A fig," I said, "for Descartes, a fart for Virgil, and his elegancies, a turd for Socrates and his philosophies."

After a few more equally strong remarks, he went on to explain his intention :

Having broken loose from my scholastic gaol, I found an aching inclination in myself to leave home and visit London —for my own diversion—and expose there the vanities and vices of the town.

And that is exactly what he did. In what was a highly competitive field as far as scandal-mongering went, he settled down to print his own paper. He had some formidable competitors. John Dunton was appealing to women readers with *The Ladies' Dictionery, A Compendium of all Knowledge for the Fair Sex.* In his first publication, Ned Ward addressed himself to the males. He called his pamphlet, *Female Policy Detected, A Pocket Piece for all Young Men to help them make a defense against the Cunning, Slyness and false Allurements of Women.* This was followed by another work, *The Night Accidents and the Whims and Follies of Staggering Stags and Strolling Strumpets.* He was soon to have opposition from Addison in *The Spectator* and Steele in *The Tatler.* But they like Daniel Defoe in his *Review* were formal, chatty and genteel. Ward was scurrilous, outspoken and obscene. If genuine copy was not available he invented it. He had no high-flown illusions about his job.

My condition is much like a strumpet—and if the reason by any reader be asked—Why do people take to such a scandalous profession as Whoring or Pamphleteering? The same answer will serve for both professions of Whores and Pamphleteers. The unhappy circumstances of a narrow fortune has forced us to do it for our sustenance.

He had his rules for writing :

One. Choose subjects as will permit a variety of observation —men who are drunkards, liars, usurers, pedlars, tapsters, mumpers, a bawdy alderman or the like.

Two. Express their natures, practices, desires with tart,

nipping kirks about their vices and miscarriages.

Three. Use only the language your readers understand and speak themselves.

It could be said that Ned Ward was the founder of the "gutter" press. In politics he was a Tory and although he wrote about the rabble of London he had no admiration for them. When he was short of scandal, he burst into verse which would have offended the people he mixed with if they had been able to read.

> Spewed out of Alleys, Gaols and Garrets,
> Fed on stinking meat and carrots,
> Liquored well with foggy ale,
> Some with bitter, mild and stale.
> Informers, labourers, brothel keepers,
> Pimps, panders, thieves and chimney sweepers,
> Unlettered, rascally and base,
> A country's danger and disgrace.

Much of what he wrote in this vein offended the Whigs. When they came into power, they thought he should be silenced for a time and punished. He was arrested and tried for libel and obscenity. On November 14, 1704, this notice appeared in *The London Gazette* :

Edward Ward, being convicted of writing, printing and publishing many scandalous and seditious libels, was ordered to stand on Wednesday next in the pillory at Charing Cross for the space of one hour between noon and two o'clock, with a paper on his head denoting his offence. And also to stand in the pillory on Thursday next near the Royal Exchange in same manner.

The pillory was one of the great daily attractions for the Londoner. This was free entertainment at its best. It cost nothing to walk by Charing Cross or the Royal Exchange and see people publicly exhibited for their wrongdoings. Moll Bunch might be on view for having used foul language to a merchant who had impeached her. She would yell out his name and tell how he had used her services when she was younger and he was a clerk in the city. Maybe it would be Nan Topley, accused of stealing money from a Dutch sea captain or Bess Grundy for having been caught

in the act of street fornication with a young gallant who had
run off without paying her and left her to be dealt with by
the Watch. As they sat in the stocks, Nan, Bess or Moll
would give Tom, Dick or Harry as good as they themselves
were receiving in the way of verbal abuse. The culprits in
pillory were pelted like figures in a pot-shot alley with
decayed fruit and rotten fish from the markets. It was all
very well for the populace to use this kind of ammunition
for the harlot and the thief. Ned Ward must have stood out
among them. His portrait shows him as a handsome man
with kindly humorous eyes, wearing a beautifully dressed
wig and a coat that would have done credit to Beau Brummell. Pope, who was not a kindly man, observed this dis-
comfiture of a fellow writer and wrote in *The Dunciad* :

As thick as eggs at Ward in pillory.

Like all good journalists, Ned Ward found copy in every
personal experience. What he heard in pillory about the
vices of London was to be used to advantage later, especially when he came to write about the women of Billingsgate and Clare Market. In his pub at Moorfields, he listened
attentively to the prostitutes telling about their nightly experiences. There were beggars who knew all the tricks of
their trade, there were petty thieves and highwaymen whose
tongues would loosen in their cups. London was a rabbit
warren of depravity. Sailors back from long voyages would
spend their time ashore whoring, drinking and telling stories
of their adventures in foreign parts. From these tales and
from what he had read in travel books, Ned Ward, to pass
the time and without the trouble of leaving London, wrote
A Trip to New England. He went, it appeared, on a ship
called *The Prudent Sarah*, but from the records it would
seem that no such vessel ever made that voyage. He informed his readers, nevertheless, that it was an offence there
to be seen kissing a woman in the street. The women were
more interested in smoking than in sex.

They smoke in bed, smoke as they knead their bread, smoke
as they cook their victuals, smoke at prayers, smoke at work,
so that their mouths stink as bad as the bowl of a sailor's pipe.

But if this trip abroad was purely imaginary, his descriptions of London life were authentic. Vice and poverty went hand in hand.

Children begged everywhere in the streets. At night they slept in doorways or in any hole or corner they could find. For a halfpenny they would say the Lord's Prayer backwards, give a new curse for every step leading to St. Pauls or "Call a Whore as many names as a Peer has titles." Their sisters and mothers made a living by begging and prostitution. At "The Sign of the Angel," a notorious pub which kept open all night, men and women slept on the floor "with their noses in conjunction with one another's arses like hogs on a dung hill."

In the first copy of *The London Spy*, Ned Ward described his arrival in London.

> I pursued my journey on foot and the second day arrived in the Metropolis, with as much wonder and amazement as the Hatford fiddler at Old Nick's Palace. I had not long passed through Aldgate when I met an old schoolfellow. He was tricked up with as much gaiety as a dancing master on a ball day. He would needs prevail on me to dine at a tavern nearby, a happy opportunity which I most readily embraced, being an utter stranger to the town.

This tavern was the first of many that Ned Ward was to visit during the remainder of his life in London. It was full of people who seemed to be well acquainted with his friend. They were in a spacious room, drinking, posturing and chattering so loudly that Ned Ward's questions to his friend could not be heard any more than if "they were ladies' farts." He asked his friend what his occupation was in the city. This conversation took place :

Friend: Come aside a little and I'll tell you. A pinch of snuff?
Ward: No, thank you. Tell me how you have prospered so well in this great city.
Friend: I'll give you my story. When I came to town, I studied a little physic at the University and got some knowledge of surgery. Most of the people you see here are my patients. You have observed them carefully?
Ward: Yes.
Friend: They are all lechers. They are seldom free from Clap, Pox and Shankers. They pay me as generously for their

cures as a wealthy spinster would for a night's recreation
with a lusty young rake she fancied.

The doctor, a man of the world, went on to describe some
of the other people in the room. There was a highwayman,
"as resolute a fellow as ever cocked a pistol on the road,"
who "feared nobody, except the hangman." He was one of
the doctor's best clients. He was most industrious in his
profession and as generous as a prince. He kept three handsome young wenches at his beck and call. The doctor explained :

> They had whores for their mothers, thieves for their fathers—
> and bawds for their tutors. My highwayman friend counts
> them good cattle if they each calve once a year. I render him
> much service and am well paid for my work.

A young man who had just come in had married an heiress and was worth £10,000. The doctor explained.

> He stinks as strong of Orange water as a Spaniard does of
> garlic. A brisk young dame who has married an old merchant
> for his money maintains him to supply the defects of her hus-
> band. Dines every night in this tavern, stirs nowhere without
> his coach, has his fencing master, dancing master and French
> master. He is so prodigal that he won't wash his hands in
> anything but the finest orange water.

As Ned Ward sat entranced at what he was seeing, an
idea got up on its elbow in his mind. He would write about
such characters as these and expose their vices and follies.
An elderly man was smoking an Indian pipe. The doctor
knew all about him. He had a toothpick made from the
claws of an American humming bird. He used it like a rake
and would demonstrate how he could pick four teeth at a
time. There was a publisher who kept a harem out of the
profits he made from starving authors. He was talking to
a parson who was "writing a work for the Church's glory,
a mess of good, hot Protestant porridge to scald the Pope."
There was an impromptu singer who could make up a
rhyme on the spur of the moment. He was declaiming in a
sing-song voice about writers and actors. The only line Ned
Ward could hear amid the hubbub was :

> their droles and their farces
> Are as bald as their arses.

Everybody in the room was laughing, talking, drinking, posturing and miming. For a young man fresh from the country it was an experience to be cherished. All that he saw and heard was soon to appear in the pages of *The London Spy*. As they walked from the Aldgate tavern towards the city, the doctor pointed out a shop window where four "provoking damsels" sat smiling sweetly at passers-by. Ned Ward stopped to observe them. They wore dresses of black velvet, with golden fringes. He thought they were parson's daughters who had borrowed their fathers' pulpit clothes.

The doctor knew better. The shop was a hairdresser's and the demure young ladies were prostitutes whose fee was a minimum of a guinea. They sat as "decoys for purse proud fops who might want their periwigs curled and perfumed." "A fashionable hairdresser's shop in London," the doctor said, "is as seldom without a number of whores in the window as St. Paul's is without a parson." Ned Ward wished to speak to the young women but the doctor advised him against this. Anyhow, he had business to attend. He had to call at "The Widow's Coffee House," where he had some patients. "They are," he said, "a little in my debt and—if last night threw some lusty cullions in their way, they may by chance make me satisfaction."

It was now dusk. They walked along to Cheapside, down a dark alley and climbed a steep staircase to a room. This was a much more extraordinary establishment that the Aldgate tavern or the hairdresser's shop. They were greeted at the top of the stairs by an old lady holding a lighted candle. She was shouting for her servant girl. "She's lately come out of the country," she said. "All she does is stand staring about her. She's as much out of place here as a whoremaster in a convent."

It was obvious to Ned Ward that he was now being introduced to his first London brothel. The old lady's language was so bawdy that even he was shocked. He described the scene:

> With this sort of talk, she ushered us into the coffee-room where, at the corner of a large table lay a large open bible, with her spectacles on the page opened, I observed, on the

Epistles of St. Paul. Next it was a quartern jug, full of some potent brew. On the floor beside her was a large green chamber pot. Next the wall was a clock, as silent as a corpse in a coffin, more for ornament than use. Above a commode, adorned with a scarlet top cloth, was an Abstract of the Acts of Parliament against drinking, swearing and all forms of vice.

The doctor suggested that before talking to the girls they should have a drink. The old lady addressed Ned Ward :

Sir, I perceive you are a stranger. I have an excellent distillation of my own preparation which some of my customers have given the name—AQUA VENERIS. It will restore a man of three score to the virility of thirty. After drinking two glasses an elderly person has found himself as randy as a young stallion. It is much in demand. I sell it to most citizens' wives in this area. They are seldom without it in their closets to encourage their husbands near bedtime.

While the doctor and Ned Ward were sampling this drink, "two mortal angels, as nimble as squirrels," came bouncing into the room. In all his writing, Ned Ward was conscious of women's garments. Over and over again, he describes them in as much detail as if he had been a fashion correspondent. It was so with the two young whores in "The Widows' Coffee House."

Their under petticoats were of white dimity, finished in Turkey work, like a fool's doublet in red, green and yellow. Their pin-up coats were of Scots braid, embellished with bugle lace. Their gowns were of printed calico. They were dressed to the best advantage, as if they were churchwarden's daughters on an Easter Sunday.

The doctor invited the girls to join him in a drink. Ned Ward was quiet, taking in all the conversation and wondering how two attractive and demure young women could belong to such a house as this. He was soon to learn that they were as bawdy in their talk and manners as the mistress of the brothel. When they had taken a fair quantity of the strong drink, they "could no longer restrain their modesty." They lifted their dimity petticoats and displayed their charms "with as many vagaries as a young monkey would with a mouse on its tail." They had been well tutored in "The Whores' Initiating Club," which young Ned Ward, then only twenty-five, was to visit later when he began to find his own way round London. When the party had grown merry, the doctor mentioned a slight matter of business. Had the girls been busy lately? They replied that trade had been very good. "Then," said the doctor politely, "perhaps you could pay the arrears due from your last misfortune?" This modest request brought a tirade of abuse from the prettiest of the girls.

> May the Lord confound you for a twat-scouring pimp. I owe you nothing. Have I not always paid you as generously as any women of quality? Have I not paid you as much for your services as any girl of my profession as trades between here and Temple Bar?

The doctor was trying to placate this vixen when "what was seemingly a sober citizen" entered the room. The girls greeted him as a welcome customer. Ned Ward and the doctor were completely ignored. There was business to be done.

"The Mistress of Debauchery" called to her maid servant and asked if there were any rods in the house, to which the country girl replied that she had "bought sixpennyworth yesterday." The two young women knew what was demanded of them. When they had been supplied with rods, they flew upstairs, followed by the sober citizen. The doctor explained that this highly respectable looking man was known in the profession as a "a flogging cullie." "It is a peculiar whim of the English," the doctor said. "The French call it, 'Le Vice Anglais.' That citizen likes to flog the girls when they are naked and will often let them scourge him till they have laid his lechery."

So ended young Ned Ward's first day in the big city. And so began *The London Spy*, the most scurillous and bawdy of all publications which were so eagerly read in the taverns and coffee houses of the city.

7

"THE LONDON SPY"

> I think it good plain English to call a fraud a fraud,
> To call a spade a spade and to call a bawd a bawd.

Ned Ward would have agreed with those lines by John Taylor, "The Water Poet." The popularity of *The London Spy* was due entirely to its plain speaking. It began as little more than a guide to the seamier side of London life. After a few editions had appeared, Ned Ward told his readers about the origin of his publication.

> I pop'd it into a cautious world as an angler does his bait among wary fish, who have oft been pricked in their nibbling. Finding the public snapping up what I write with greediness, I purpose to continue as long as they give me encouragement.

Six months later he wrote :

> I have now experienced what operations my writings have upon the public. Some they please, some they vex, some praise 'em, some damn 'em, some thank me, others threaten me. I have made in a few months as much noise in this town as if for seven years I had scribbled droles for Bartholomew Fair or been the renowned author of Whittington-Cat.

The story of Dick Whittington and his cat was no more remarkable that the success of Ned Ward in London. For the most of thirty years, he held his readers firmly. No man with eyes and ears open, he believed, could walk twenty yards in a London street without finding something of interest. He had an insatiable curiosity about all human behaviour, especially in its relationship to men and women. In his own fashion, he preached the gospel that Freud was to expound centuries later.

If his mind ran mainly on sex and bawdiness, it was because that is what he found around him everywhere. Many

Londoners drank and fornicated, swore and lived riotously. His experience was that the women were as lewd and lustful as the men. With his jovial manner and eternal good humour, he made friends easily and could draw people out. It was a common question in the taverns and coffee houses to ask a friend if he had seen the latest edition of *The London Spy*. It contained always something of topical interest. One issue would deal with a visit to Bedlam, the first lunatic asylum in Europe. Another would feature the Stock Exchange or St. James's Park.

He was the first to inform Londoners that members of the Stock Exchange had their private brothel. "Where there is money," he wrote, "there will always be beautiful women." The Exchange was a busy prosperous place. Outside it quacks sold remedies for every ailment. In a large room upstairs sat groups of attractive women with "voices as sweet as sirens." A well-dressed man walked about "with as much pace and gravity as a snail over a cabbage leaf." He was the keeper of the seraglio. His duty was to find women of good appearance and with good manners who would entertain the city gentlemen when the work of the day was over. The ladies wore starched "pin-folds" and looked respectable and demure.

It was an honour to be selected for inclusion in this collection of beauties. A prominent city man could not be seen in any of the ordinary brothels. The private seraglio was, therefore, a necessity. Outwardly, the ladies were supposed to be selling lace or linen but this was merely a cloak to hide their more important duties. Everything was conducted in the most genteel manner. It had been known for a girl to forsake the harem of George I for the more rarified atmosphere of the Stock Exchange. The pretty daughter of a poor country parson could always find work there. So could the attractive widow or forsaken mistress of a speculator who had lost his money. This was London prostitution at its highest level. Bedlam was the reverse on the lowest possible scale.

Ned Ward described how he went there one day and was admitted through a great iron gate by a brawny man who was leaning on a money box for some unknown reason.

Perhaps for a small contribution he would supply information about the facilities to be found inside. Inside there was a great rattling of chains, drumming on doors, ranting and singing. A non-stop talker was telling the visitors that he "had an army of eagles at his command" and that the man in the moon was a rascal. He had asked this "Chief Lunatic of the Universe" to send him a case of claret. The reply was that the heavenly cellars were empty because there was a shortage of supply. Judging by the redness of some of the faces around him, the man said, this was obviously not so in London.

Ned Ward was less interested in the inmates than he was in the visitors. He wrote :

> I could not help but remark on the looseness of the spectators. Whores there were of every rank—from the velvet scarf to the Scotch plaid petticoat. There was a suitable Jill for every Jack. Every freshcomer was soon engaged in an amour. They came in singles and went away in pairs. Bedlam is as great a convenience in London as the Long Cellar in Amsterdam, where any visitor may get a purge for his penis. Bedlam is an almshouse for madmen, a showing room for whores, a sure market-place for lechers, a dry resting place for loiterers and pickpockets.

There was a gayer and more elegant section of amorous life to be seen in London. The merchants' wives and daughters met their lovers in and around Covent Garden, sometimes in the flower market, sometimes in the church. The court ladies found St. James's Park a more suitable rendezvous. The editor of *The London Spy* observed what went on there :

> I went into the park about the time when the court ladies raise their limbs from their downy couches and walk into the Mall to refresh their charming bodies with the cooling breezes of the gilded evening. I could not have chosen a luckier minute, for the brightest stars of creation were here, with such a state of majesty that their graceful deportment bespoke them goddesses. A band in the distance was playing softly. I could have gazed for ever with inexpressible delight on every lovely face, with due regard to Heaven for importing to us such a display of celestial harmony in the beautiful and curious of all living creatures—Women.

But although Ned Ward was fascinated by the splendour of the ladies, he was not impressed by "the creeping humility of their cringing worshippers." To him they all looked effeminate, "a parcel of fawning fops." He asked himself a number of pertinent questions.

Did these overdressed emasculated creatures not realise that women were decreed by Heaven to be men's inferiors? Were they educated among monkeys who, it is well known, give in all cases full pre-eminence to their females? Things were different not far away in Duke Humphrey's Walk. The exclusive part of the park was like the royal enclosure at Ascot, reserved for the ladies and gentlemen who had access to the palace. Less important but more affluent dames paraded in Duke Humphrey's Walk. The men there were the bold masculine types, who had conferred on themselves the ranks of captain or major. Ned Ward made enquiries and was told :

> This is where a city lady as rich as she is lewd may furnish herself with a lover if she will allow him good clothes, three meals a day and money for wine. If she likes him she need not fear losing him as long as she has money. Only poverty in the old mistress will bring them here to seek a new one.

A group of these gentlemen were standing underneath a tree, waiting to be bought "like stallions at a Yorkshire fair." Ducks were frisking in a pond, "standing on their heads and showing as many tricks as a tumbler at a fair." The band was still playing softly in the distance. As dusk descended on this sylvan scene, the ladies had made their choice. Couples walked off arm in arm together under the trees to find quiet places where they could make their preliminary embraces. "Pensive lovers," Ned Ward wrote, "were whispering their affections to their newly found mistresses and breathing out sighs of their future happiness."

All this might be considered too great an emphasis on sex life in the past, were it not for the fact that much the same is happening today. Women with money still buy lovers for themselves, men still pay for the favours of women. Such transactions were perhaps carried out with more subtlety and graciousness in the eighteenth century. But London then in this respect was much the same as it is now. As he walked from St. James's Park by the Half Moon Tavern towards Covent Garden, Ned Ward overtook "a number of lady birds, armed against the assaults of Satan with bibles and common prayer books." He enquired if this was a usual custom and who these "pious creatures" were. He was told that they were the young wives and daughters of merchants. "They are in search," said a market women, "of what all young females desire most." The market women were "jolly, red-faced dames in blue aprons and straw hats." They knew what was going on. As Ned Ward stood talking to them, a group of young men approached. They followed the ladies into the church. As it was in Bedlam and St. James's Park, each Jack found his Jill. This was the place where they came each evening to make their assignations. *The London Spy* reported :

> Covent Garden market and church hide more faults of wives and daughters that pretended visits to cousins at the other end of the town. If a husband should ask his wife, "Where have you been?" the answer is "I've been to evening prayers." If the question be asked in early morning—when many amorous trysts take place—the lady will say, "I took a walk in the market, to smell the sweet scent of the herbs and flowers."

After Covent Garden, the roving journalist of *The London Spy* found copy at Billingsgate. At the end of a narrow lane, there was a pub which "stank of stale sprats and piss." He heard the sound of women's voices and went inside.

> Around a fire sat a tattered assembly of fat flat caps, with their fish baskets on their laps. Every one had her nipperkin of ale and brandy. Every one of them was as slender in the waist as a Dutch skipper in the buttocks. Their cheeks were as plump as an infant's arse.

One of these ladies looked at the stranger and said :

> God save you, honest master, will you pledge me a toast?

Not knowing how to react to this request, Ned Ward spoke to a man, who advised him not to join the company of "these saucy-tongued whores" or they "would tease him to death." This remark was heard. One of the women let go a torrent of her best Billingsgate :

You white-livered son of a Fleet Street bumseller. I know your kind—begot on a chair at noon-day between Ludgate Hill and Temple Bar. Who is it you call whore? I'm not like the mangy streetwalker who brought you into the world. I wouldn't waste my piss on you if you were lying on fire at my feet.

This was the kind of language that most readers of *The London Spy* knew and understood. From the fishwives of Billingsgate, Ned Ward went to observe the life of Wapping. He described the swaying hackney coaches as they rattled along the narrow cobbled streets, barely missing the corners of some of the jutting houses with their creaking signs and overhanging balconies. When two coaches got interlocked, the drivers cursed each other with the most profane oaths. The life of the pedestrian was in constant danger.

All along Thameside there was bustling life and excitement. Watermen wrangled with passengers about fares, apprentices and shop girls huddled close together in boats. On the river there were "Barges, Cockboats, Bum-boats, Pinnaces and Yawls." Boisterous young men had ladles which they filled with water and doused each other while their girl friends yelled in merriment at the scene. Young sailors caught girls in the street and kissed them till they screamed and were not unwillingly dragged or carried bodily into the dark rooms of a tavern. In a fairground nearby one of the attractions was an Irishman whose performance was to eat an aged rooster alive. Ned Ward quoted the advertisement :

The Irishman that ate the live cock at Islington and another since on the 15th of June is to eat another at Newington Butts in the Borough on Tuesday next, with feathers, bones and garbage. Any person may see this, paying twopence of Admission.

On his way back from this jolly entertainment, Ned Ward passed by St. Paul's, where the three hundred feet of the new spire was being built. Visitors to the city as well as the Londoners were watching the work in progress. The craftsmen on the job were going leisurely about their labour. In what we would call today their "break," they sat drinking pints of ale carried from the nearest tavern by their assistants. A young bricklayer's "mate" was entertaining the onlookers with a bawdy song. The ever watchful private eye of Ned Ward was wide open.

In the churchyard, bookstalls and booksellers are as thick as pedlars at any fair. Nearby is a picture-print seller's where smutty drawings are much in demand. Crowds gather round the Musick shops where the apprentices are scratching the strings of fiddles. The visitors stare at the greatness of the building and watch the stone-cutters at work. The Cathedral is slow a-building and the workmen often stop to rest.

In Jonathon's coffee shop, there was this notice for all to read :

This may certify, all my Loving Masters and Ladies, that on Wednesday, being the 26th day of April, at Dame Butterfield's at Mobb's Hole, will be a house warming, where all my loving Friends shall be kindly entertained with Calf roasted whole, and a Flitch of Bacon roasted whole, and other Varieties with Musick: And also being an old Hunter, I shall accommodate you with Six Brass Horns, sounding delightful harmony. So hoping, my delightful Masters and Ladies, all Friends and Acquaintances, will be pleased to honour me with their Company. And, as I am in duty bound, shall ever return your thanks and remains Yours, obliged to serve you, Susanna Butterfield.

This was too good an opportunity to miss. Dame Butterfield was clearly a woman after Ned Ward's own heart. On the appointed day he took advantage of her open invitation and went to the housewarming at Mobb's Hole. He was not disappointed. This was "Merrie England" at its best.

Beaux were in boots black as jet, with a bayonet or short scymater hanging from their belts. The ladies were tyed up in Safeguards beknotted with Tuppeny Taffety. Hackneys and Hunters, Coaches and Carts, Waggons and Tumblers filled the roads, as if all London had been going to encamp at Mobb's Hole. The ragtag and bobtail of the town were there, jumbling against City quality, from a Beau to a Booby, from a Lady of a Merchant to a thumb-ringed Alewife. Some sat on the grass, some danced to the bagpipes. Others climbed like monkeys into trees. The major part of a calf was roasting on a wooden spit.

We have nowhere a better account of how Londoners enjoyed themselves than in this record of the inauguration of Dame Butterfield's new tavern. In an outhouse, a fiddler was playing and young people were singing and dancing to the tune of "Now Ponder well you parents, dear," a top-of-the-pops warning to older folk that youth would have its fling. And what a fling it was that day. There were wild pursuits by lusty young men after lovely girls making pretended struggles to escape. The pipes of Pan were playing. Cupid was shooting his darts in every direction. Between the singing and the dancing, people were cramming down as much veal and ham as they could eat. Ale and wine was being supplied generously by a dozen serving men and women. Everything was free. All around there were quiet green places where lovers could enjoy themselves. The frolics went on till long after midnight. Ned Ward left Mobb's Hole with the sound of a post horn ringing in his ears and went home to write about this joyful day and bring his copy to the printer.

If he was concerned largely with the more convivial side of life, Ned Ward turned his attention now and then to more serious subjects. On these few occasions he became a contemporary commentator who has put many historians deeply in his debt. His account of Dryden's death and funeral is an example. He gave details as truthful as they are sordid about the poet's final illness and death, of how his lameness came from flesh growing over his toe nails and his refusal to have his leg amputated. He described the funeral: The hearse was drawn by six stately Flanders horses, with plumes of black feathers. The procession was led "by two Beadles of the College in Mourning Cloaks and Hatbands, with the Heads of their staffs wrapped in black crepe." The coaches which carried the mourners to Westminster were each drawn by six horses.

In this order, the Nobility and the Gentry attended the Hearse to the Abbey, where the Choir, assisted by the best Masters in England sang an Epicedium. When the last funeral rights had been performed by one of the Prebends, Dryden was honourably interred between Chaucer and Cowley.

From the solemnity of this occasion, "jovial, brutal, vulgar Ned Ward" could move to the lowest depth of coarseness. "The Secret Clubs of London," the work by which he is best known, was so obscene in parts that he decided not to put his own name to it. By this time he had become a citizen of some importance. *The Poetical Register*, a biographical dictionary, had this entry:

> Mr. Edward Ward is a voluminous poet. Of late years he has kept a public house in the city (but in a genteel way) and with his Wit, Good Humour—and Good Liquor—affords his guests a pleasurable Entertainment, especially the High Church Party, which is composed of men of his principles, and to whom he is very much obliged for their constant support.

If there was something genteel about the pub where Ned Ward was landlord, that term could not be applied to his stories about the London clubs which were then becoming such a feature of London life. He had begun to take as much interest in them as "a maid at a Gossiping where married women are talking bawdy."

8

THE SECRET CLUBS

Birds of a Feather—

There were many queer male birds and an assortment of tawdry-feathered hens in the clubs Ned Ward wrote about. Some of them belonged to the lunatic fringe of London life. Ned himself was greatly influenced by the moon. He liked to see it shining over the city when he made the nightly rounds of the pubs and brothels. There were times when of necessity he stumbled home in the early hours of the morning. Like many other Londoners he liked to see a bright moon in the sky when he went aroving. Because of the danger of footpads, it was the custom for many clubs to hold their meetings on moonlit nights. It was not surprising, therefore, that Ned Ward made this dedication :

To the Luciferous and Sublime Lunatick, the Emperor of the Moon, Convenor of the Tides, Corrector of all Female Constitutions and Metropolitan of all Revolving Cities, I dedicate this Work.

I take the opportunity of expressing my Gratitude to your Illustrious Highness for the Wonderful Favours I have received at late hours from the Refulgence of your Throne. From many an adversary posted at the corner of a Street have I happily escaped through the Pleasing Benefit of your Light. Many a dirty Aqueduct have I straggled over in the rays of your Divine Splendour.

I am sensible, Your Noble Lucidity, that you may wonder why I have chosen you as a Patron. Having read somewhere in the works of a late celebrated Poet that "Great Wits to Madness nearly are allied," I concluded there would be no great difference between me and a Lunatick—and so I thought that the Lunacies I write about are a proper subject to entertain Your Highness.

We shall never know how far Ned Ward stretched his imagination when he wrote about "The Secret Clubs of London." There is no doubt that such meeting places as he described were to be found throughout the city. It is certain that many of them were what today we would call the underworld of London. There were, of course, highly respectable clubs like White's, Brooke's, Almack's and Boodles where the elite met to drink, talk and gamble. There were clubs, like the Kit-Kat, for intellectuals. Ned Ward would have been blackballed at the first go in any of them. His inclination was to poke fun at these august institutions. There were neither his cup of coffee nor his pint of ale. Give him the taverns where the less respectable citizens were to be found. Some of what he wrote about them may have had an element of fiction but all of it was based on some personal experience or from information received.

The London Spy had brought him almost as many enemies as it had readers. His revelations about certain clubs in the city made him detested by their members. It was all very well for "The Mollies Club" to meet privately and indulge in homosexual practices. It was a different matter when an account of their proceedings appeared in print and was read in every coffee house in the city. Few Londoners knew that there was such an institution as "The Mollies Club" in their midst until Ned Ward told them. Even he had to pull his punches a little.

In the majority of cases the meeting places of the clubs were mentioned. All we are told about the rendezvous of "The Mollies" is that they met in a tavern which could not be mentioned, since "to put an address on the house would give it an odious name." We learn that the leading lights of "The Mollies" were people of influence. It is unlikely that Ned Ward ever attended one of their gatherings. He would not have been a welcome guest. Like all gossip writers from Pepys to our own day, he had his sources of inside information. Most of "The Mollies" were men of good social standing who found their boy friends among the lower classes. Some of the members were actors and writers. One of them may well have produced these lines :

The Devil's come a-Pounding at the door.
He raps at first and then he soundly beats.
Within, Ned Ward, who through the keyhole peeps.
Expecting Bailiff, Debtor or some Whore,
He pox'd or bilk't a day or two before.

From this it will be clear that Mr. Ward was by no
means popular everywhere. He had this to say about "The
Mollies" :

> They are so far depraved from all masculine deportment
> that they fancy themselves women, initiating in themselves
> all the vanities that custom has reconciled to the female sex,
> affecting to speak, walk, tattle, curtsey, scold each other and
> mimic all manners of effeminacy.

When it came to writing about thieves, beggars and liars,
he showed much consideration. He liked the company of
bawdy women, whether they plied their trade at the Stock
Exchange, the fashionable hairdressers' shops, in Bedlam,
Billingsgate or Clare Market. "The Mollies" were completely outside his pale.

> It is the pleasure of these citizens to ape women in vulgar
> mime and word. One of them will appear in a nightdress,
> sit on a commode, curl his hair and pretend he is preparing
> for bed. Another will play the character of a woman going
> through the pains of parturition, while another will dress as
> a country midwife to see offspring safely delivered. The first
> requisite for membership is a complete contempt for the
> beauty of women and the belief that amorous intercourse
> between man and man is more desirable than any pleasure
> Venus has to offer.

A complete antithesis to "The Mollies" was the "Beaux
Club," which met at the Dog Tavern in Drury Lane. The
members here were all "Lechers, Old Stallions and young
Whoremasters." They met at noon to eat, drink and talk
about their love affairs. Their clubroom was as well furnished with cosmetics as if it had belonged to Beau Brummell
or Beau Nash. In this case, Ned Ward got his facts at first
hand. He was able to describe the setting in detail

> At the upper end of the clubroom is a sideboard which is
> constantly furnished with at least a dozen flannel muck-

finders, folded up for removing all elusive specks of dust from the attire. Next to these is an Olive box, full of the best perfumed powders and three mighty combs. Round the edge of the table is strewn by way of garnish a collection of patches, toothpickers, with tweezers, pomatums, pastes and washes. The members are no sooner met than they grow as busy as so many stage players dizening their faces before appearing in a comedy.

While this was going on there was lively chatter and much laughter and badinage. Women and their charms were the sole topic. The food was brought in, the members took their places at the table and the proceedings were opened by the chairman.

Chairman: Pray be seated, gentlemen. Let me see. Yes. Our menu today consists of pig's head with the snout cut off.

Member: May I ask, sir, why the snout has been cut off?

Chairman: I am informed by our landlord that he thought it seemly to be in the fashion. He says pigs should be snoutless.

Member: A pox on the son of a dripping pan. Does he now know that all our mistresses love nothing better than a long snout on a man.

With such merry quips and jests, the members of the Beaux Club drank and talked throughout the afternoon. But there was much more entertainment to follow. Wigs were powdered and rearranged. More wine was drunk. Some talked, others played cards. In the evening they sauntered slowly to the theatre to keep their appointments, arriving there before the curtain has risen on the final act. By this time, their harlots were lined up like a beauty chorus in the foyer. They "had eaten their stews, been laced up in their stays and had generally adorned themselves." There was no competition since each one had her own man. Seeing the play was unimportant. The gentlemen would move inside to applaud the actors at the end of the performance. The ladies would gossip agreeably among themselves.

These girls knew their place. For a time they would listen to the bawdy talk of the men and pretend to be shocked. Then they would graciously retire to their respective apartments. The gentlemen would go to a gaming club. Before midnight they would join their ladies and remain with them till morning. This was the greater part of twenty-four hours in the day of a member of "The Beaux Club." It is not surprising that they met only once each week.

In complete contrast to the comparative luxurious surroundings of the "Beaux" and "The Mollies," "The Thieves' Club" met in an underground hide-out in Blackfriars, the address of which was understandably a secret. This establishment was run by a most highly respected "Receiver," who ruled with an iron hand. He paid well for the stolen goods brought to him. If the law put any of his clients temporarily out of business, he saw that their girl friends were kept in funds. He would deal only with the elite of the profession. He kept good liquor, would lend money if business was bad but would trust only those who knew how to exercise their talents and had chosen their right vocation in life. He liked men who worked hard, did not go to excess in drink or sex and got "a living honestly by their skill." Ned Ward discovered that "most honest thieves will talk—like any usurer or banker in the city—about their trade with pride."

He enquired from one member of the club if business was good and was told that he had been fortunate to earn £300 on the previous night. This conversation took place:

Ward: How did you earn this money?
Thief: With the help of one of my Misses.
Ward: But how?
Thief: This Miss of mine was got with child by a young nobleman through no fault of her own. He died of a pox and this Miss of mine—who can mimic like any actress—is now chambermaid to his grandmother. I'm a honest thief.
Ward: I know you are. But tell me more.
Thief: I'll tell you all. This old lady when she got in her cups would talk about the lovers she had when she was young and would ramble away to my Miss about men. Then she would ask for more punch. And when she had all she could take, my Miss brought me in last night and

said I was one of the young men the old lady had known
when she was a girl. She said she remembered me well but
was too tired to talk and wanted to sleep. So we took the
£300—which was honest gotten money.

After a few editions had appeared, *The History of the
Secret Clubs* was as popular as *The London Spy*. It covered
an extensive field, even if some of the "clubs" visited did
not come under the strict definition of that word. A few
of them were merely taverns where birds of a feather met.
The headquarters of "The Whore's Initiating Club" was
in Coleyard Gateway at Drury Lane. It was the recognised
rendezvous for procuresses, like Catherine Hayes, Moll
King, "Mother" Stanhope and Mrs. Goadby, who was
used by Hogarth as the model for the old bawd in "The
Harlot's Progress."

If a young girl wished to meet any of these ladies she
would find them any afternoon drinking brandy and talking business. She would be critically examined for her looks
and manner and would be accepted for training if she
passed muster. There was no percentage offering work to a
completely unsuitable candidate. Even if she had what it
took, an inexperienced girl had to learn the tricks of the
trade. The information Ned Ward gleaned at Coleyard
Gateway came from "a withered lady in the autumn of her
years who had given a universal distribution of her own
youthful favours." Her job now was to instruct "country
wenches or maids out of service" who wanted to take up
the profession. She would show them how "to sweeten an
old lecher and how to keep a customer once she had got
him." Even more important for the novice was to learn
how to find clients. The withered old lady was like an
actress who could no longer perform but could impart the
benefit of her long experience. As there was always an
audience for the theatre, so was there a continuous demand
for the services of her best pupils. It was, however, a buyer's
market with no scarcity of supply. There was always on
the street some kind of man on the look-out for a whore he
fancied. The instructress would take one girl at a time round
the city centre and show her the best beats. She would
explain to her that she must walk slowly, stop and look into

windows, then move on again. She would tell her how to give smiling encouragement to a shy young man and how to talk to him if and when conversation began.

If the girl was approached and was unsuccessful, she would be told where possibly she had gone wrong. Every prospective client required different treatment. He might be "a demure little spark" who was lonely and wanted company. Around Coleyard Gateway, Ned Ward noticed "rakes, gamesters, liverymen, a brawny butcher equipped with a freshly combed and powdered wig from a second-hand shop in London Lane." One might be a small shop-keeper from Chancery Lane, a lawyer's clerk or a poorly paid apprentice. Some would haggle with a girl about the price, some would not raise the question of money at all, the more particular ones would "make a selection as carefully as a dandy would buying a new set of frills." The members of "The Whore's Initiating Club" held out high hopes for a girl of good appearance who could deal with such a variety of characters and circumstances. She might persuade Jack Harris to put her on his exclusive "List of Covent Garden Ladies." She might, like the elite of the profession—Fanny Murray, Martha Rae or Nancy Parsons —become the mistress of a Member of Parliament or a lord. The ladies who met to drink their brandy daily at Coleyard Gateway firmly believed that they were offering a useful service.

Ned Ward's first intention was to select six clubs for his pamphlets. The demand, however, became so great that he added another ten. The number finally increased to thirty-two. Some were the meeting places more for eccentrics than bawds.

"The Liar's Club" met weekly at a tavern in Westminster. It was composed mainly of retired professional men from in and around Whitehall. Before being admitted to membership, a candidate had to prove that he could tell a colossal lie at some length. After lunch the "liar" of the day got up to make his contribution. If he failed to come up to expectation, he was obliged to buy a gallon of wine of the chairman's choice and give the servants of the house five shillings. The lie would often be about an amorous adventure or good luck at cards, horse racing or some other recreation. All the members asked for was a tall story par excellence. They got good value for their money the day Ned Ward was there. After they had eaten well, the chairman rapped the table and said, "I pray silence, gentlemen, for Sir Harry Flount." Sir Harry, an old roué, did not speak about his favourite subject—women. Ned Ward reported his story in full.

Gentlemen, one day in the tropics, I had a mind to go fishing. Taking with me one of my Indian servants to bear me company, we came to a large river where, he told me, there was a plenitude of great fish. Walking along the banks to find a shady place, I got among a bed of osiers to keep me from the scorching heat. When I entered upon my pastime, I immediately got a bite. But as ill luck would have it, I was wearing a feathered head-dress, much used in India. As this feathered turban, Gentlemen, was moving among the osiers, a great swinging hawk, no doubt taking my head-dress for some strange kind of bird, came swooping down and with a most furious stroke at me, snatched away my turban. Under this surprise I dropped my angling rod—and lost my fish. Having, however, suffered no physical damage, I continued till I had another bite. This fish proved to be so heavy that my Indian servant had to go into the water to fetch it out.

You'll excuse me, Gentlemen, I can now feel the heat of that tropical day and feel a little dry. Your very good healths, Gentlemen.

And now to continue. The bite proved such a great fish which had gorged my hook that I was forced—much against my will—to cut him open. I found, Gentlemen, that I had taken not one but SEVEN fish. The first of these had been swallowed by a bigger fish, these two had been swallowed by a third fish, then by a fourth and by a fifth and a sixth which had been swallowed by the great fish I had caught. So, Gentlemen, I had caught a nest of SEVEN FISH at one fortunate cast of my angling rod.

This story brought a round of applause but Sir Harry had not finished.

Pray, Gentlemen, let me continue. That is not all my story. On my way home—to my great surprise and with unerring aim, the swinging hawk dropped my feathered hat, which fell on my noddle as neatly as if it had been placed there by any London haberdasher. I came away, Gentlemen, reflecting that fish are as gluttonous as the esteemed members of the London Beefsteak Club and that birds of prey have a sense of honesty which, I regret to say, I have often found wanting in many gentlemen in this city of London.

"The Market Women's Club" was a gathering after Ned Ward's own heart. The members who met daily in an ale house near Clare Market told stories as bawdy as any that could be heard anywhere in London. They had an enormous capacity for consuming liquor. They were of all ages.

The younger ones are rosy sunburnt wenches from villages who come riding into town like kettle drummers between their full-bellied panniers, well stuffed with good fruit. They are as free in their morals as a goat or a sheep and like nothing better than a good ram. They look upon her as a weak sister who doesn't lift her skirt three or four times every day or drink two quarts of ale.

The landlord of the tavern where the market women met was an eccentric character who liked "discursive arguments on divers subjects." He told Ned Ward that if a woman would stare at three or four lighted candles for half an hour wearing blue spectacles, she could consume any given amount of intoxicating drink. When a Cheapside merchant challenged this statement, the landlord offered a wager that he would find three of his customers who would drink a hogshead of claret at one sitting without falling asleep. The contest was duly arranged. The women put on the blue glasses, looked at the candles for the required time and sat down to the job. They asked first of all for a dish of tongues, for pipes and tobacco. Then they began on the claret, drinking, smoking and talking about other days. One of them remembered Peg Keeble who could "take more drink than any Dutch sailor when she was sixteen." Peg had a weakness for seafaring men. "She was as good a girl," one of the market women said, "as ever lost her maidenhead in a hammock."

The session lasted till the early hours of the morning. The men who had been supplied with as much strong drink as they could take retired one by one. The three women kept on smoking, drinking and talking incessantly. At five o'clock they called for a quart of mulled wine. "They were," wrote Ned Ward, "still physically, mentally and hydraulically perfect." By this time the sunburnt wenches from the country had arrived at Clare Market with their produce.

The Cheapside merchant who had lost his wager met the three contestants on his way to business at Clare Market. Apart from finding them merry, inclined to dance and roar out bawdy songs, he could see nothing unusual in their behaviour. It is a matter for speculation whether or not the success of their marathon effort was due to staring at lighted candles through blue spectacles. It is more likely that these lusty market women had the best of all English qualities, a happy contented nature, an independent spirit and an iron constitution. They were the type of Londoner in which Ned Ward took the most delight. He was even more at ease with them than he was at "The Beefsteak Club," which met at "The Sign of the Imperial Phiz" at Old Jewry. The chairman there was an Irish comedian called Eastcourt, who was then the rage of the town. He had a silver gridiron round his neck as his chain of office. He sang a song of his own composition :

> Of all the parts of noble beef,
> Given by God for man's relief.
> The juicy rump is still the best,
> Beneath the tail and horned crest.

Ned Ward had little to report about the most famous wining and dining club of the period, "The Kit-Kat," which met at "The Sign of the Cat and Fiddle," a coffee house in the Strand near Temple Bar. It took its name from a pastry cook, Christopher Catt, whose pies and tarts were devoured greedily by the members of the club, most of them politicians and poets who wrote odes in favour of royalty. Ned Ward had only this to say about them :

The refined wits of the Kit-Kat Club feed their fancies with female dainties out of respect for the Muses who are always believed to be feminine. The more masculine worthies of the Beefsteak Club, having more regard to the strength of body than the activity of mind, choose a more substantial food that might assist their limbs and recommend them to the ladies who prefer Mars' truncheon to Apollo's harp and—instead of odes—would rather have their charms commended by the caressing hugs of a strenuous lover.

Ned Ward had clearly no use for the Kit-Kat members. The Beefsteak Club was better.

> They have shown that they are wise.
> They eat good beef—not Kit-Kat pies.

More to his liking still was "The Yorkshire Club," which met every horse-fair day in "The Rounds" at Smithfield. The members here were huge rosy-cheeked north-country-men, lusty, exuberant chaps who liked good food and good drink and had plenty of money. They were much in favour with the market women.

The most prosperous of them own stallions to top the mares brought to the fair by ostlers. There is much interest and delight shown among the wenches when the noble acts are being done and the mares are squealing. The stallion owners are sought after by the better whores, who are dressed and perfumed like Court ladies and show much jealousy for the favours of the men, such as they know to be as good per-formers as their stallions. The lesser harlots must make do with the ostlers and the hackney dealers. When the Yorkshire men—the business of the day over—have drunk, ate their belliesful and made sure that their stallions have done like-wise, they will go off happily to find couches with their favourite jades.

And so week by week the daily and nightly rounds of the taverns and ale-houses went on. In Old Street there was "The Beggars Club," a collection of "Old Beards, Wooden-Legged Implorers of Charity, Sham Disabled Sea-men and Blind Gunpowder-Blasted Mumpers."

Ned Ward could rattle off lines of verse at the drop of a hat. He was so impressed by a ballad singer he met at "The Beggars' Club" that he wrote this song for him :

> Begging is an honest trade,
> That wealthy knaves despise,
> Yet rich men may be beggars made
> And we that beg may rise.

What tho' the world we make believe,
That we are maimed or lame,
'Tis now a virtue to deceive,
The rich folk do the same.

Let heavy taxes greater grow,
And we shall live to see,
That begging in a little time,
A common trade may be.

This was an age when scientific discovery was as much
in the public mind as space travel is today. The purpose of
"The Virtuoso Club," which met weekly in Cornhill was
"to propagate new whims, advance mechanical exercises
and discuss some fanciful discovery that had put a crochet
in the head of a member." One had an idea for conveying
the pure fresh air of Hampstead by subterranean pipes to
London for the benefit of all consumptive families. Another
was experimenting with a machine for turning sea brine
into a gaseous beverage "that will be wholesome to the
body and as pleasant to the palate as French brandy." A
third was of the opinion that he would find the Philosopher's Stone in the ashes of a burnt haystack. Even among
this circle, Ned Ward found an opportunity to introduce
his favourite subject—sex.

You can all but hear him whispering in the ear of a
reader :

> I know one member of the Virtuoso Club who sits each
> night in his ivory tower studying the composition of elephants'
> tusks and other bones while his young wife and her lover are
> providing him cuckold's horns downstairs.

Ned Ward wrote and published over a hundred collections of poems, pamphlets and satirical sketches. He reached
his lowest ebb of vulgarity when he dealt with "The Farters'
Club," which met, he tells us, in a tavern near Fleet Ditch.
The most obscene writings of Swift and Rabelais are like
Sunday school tracts in comparison with this unforgiveable
lapse from good taste. Some of the stories told are completely unprintable and are neither amusing nor witty. This
introduction will give some indication of what followed :

Of all the Fantastical Societies that ever took pains to make themselves stink in the nostrils of the Publick, the greatest is "The Farters' Club." For their excremental practices, they diet themselves with Cabbage, Onions, Peas and poison the air with the unsavoury flatulations with which one tries to outdo the other.

As he continued to write about these aspects of London life, the supply was obviously running low. Yet much of what he has left on record is a valuble contribution to our knowledge of how people entertained themselves in the eighteenth century, if we exclude the members of "The Farters' Club." Ward himself was a member of "The Small Coal-Man's Club."

This exclusive society assembled each Thursday above a small shop at St. James's Gate. One of the members was Sam Scott, who kept a "Musick House at Temple Gate, where he sold Harps, Fiddles, and Bories and was a great lover of the pipe and the bottle." He had three cronies, "Salisbury Joe, who was a Court barber, an Irish engraver and a Scotch writing master." Between them they smoked a pound of tobacco in an hour. Tom Britton, the founder of the club had a collection of ancient and modern music. People who saw him going about with his barrow thought he was a nobleman in disguise. "In truth," Ned Ward tells us, "he was a Small Coalman, a Lover of Learning, a Performer of Musick, a Companion for any Gentleman." This is about all in his writings that Ned Ward has to say about an intimate friend. According to his contemporaries, he was no stranger in the bawdy houses of the city. We hear nothing about his wife or family. We know that he kept taverns in different parts of the city, at Clerkenwell, Moorfields and at Gray's Inn. His only obituary notice appeared in *The Country Magazine*.

On Tuesday night died Mr. Ned Ward, famous for his poetical performances.

An account of his will was published in *Applebee's Weekly* in September, 1731. He wished to be buried at St. Pancras and not in noisy Cripplegate. He asked for a simple funeral, with one coach to convey his wife and children. His goods and chattels were to be sold to pay his just debts.

When you read his *History of the Secret Clubs*, you realise that in some respects life in London was much the same then as it is now. "The Mock Heroes' Club" might well have its counterparts today.

> This group of young Desperadoes, apprentices and clerks, met before the Watch had them out of their haunt in a tavern near the Tennis Court at the back of Lincoln's Inn. They are now to be found at "The Three Tuns" in Southwark and other kens in the neighbourhood. They fancy themselves as gentlemen adventurers and will adopt such names as Antonius Copywell or Valentine Drinkwater. They will make game of an honest country girl out to make a living on the streets but they have met their match when they were caught and scratched by some of the rapacious Amazonian harlots of Blackfriars. From one who was in this company but has repented since he got with child and married his master's daughter, I am told that it is their custom to tell tales of their escapades, of having slit noses, ravished women and slid them in barrels down Ludgate Hill. When they leave the tavern at night they will shout with wild cries, "Hey, boys, who's for scouring the Watch and breaking their lanterns? Who's for beating up whores and breaking the windows of the bawdy houses?"

No publisher has ever thought it worth while to reprint the works of Ned Ward. Yet many historians and writers refer to him often. Macaulay certainly knew all about him, so did Mayhew when he wrote his account of London life. The leader of "The Mock Heroes" may well have given Dickens the idea for the character of Sim Tappertit in *Barnaby Rudge*. Sir Harry Flount's description at "The Liars' Club" of the seven fish he caught at one bite in tropical heat has a remarkable resemblance to the tall story about the famous cricket match told to Mr. Pickwick by Mr. Jingle.

We owe, I think, to Ned Ward the term, "Billingsgate," which has lasted through the centuries to describe bad language. He refers to it in his account of "The Surly Club."

> This Society, composed of lightermen and fish porters, meet in a tavern at Billingsgate Dock. Their aim is to exercise the

spirit of contradiction and perfect one another in the use of foul talk, that they might so abuse honest passengers on the Thames or gentlemen in the streets. If a candidate for membership is unable to reel off his tongue a variety of obscene oaths, the chairman will address him with words which no whore would use in dismissing a maid for having shown too much modesty. The members of "The Surly Club" have greatly improved the language of Billingsgate by adding many new bawdy adages which they thunder out like volleys from a regiment of trainbands.

In one case at least Ned Ward seems to have been prophetic. "The Atheistical Club," which met at Cripplegate, bears an extraordinary resemblance to the "Hell-Fire Club," which was not founded till 1746, fifteen years after Ned Ward's death. He tells us that the members of the former were unbelieving profligates and libertines. So was Sir Francis Dashwood and the "monks" of "The Hell-Fire Club." One evening while a meeting of "The Atheistical Club" was in progress "a group of merry God-fearing Gentlemen who were taking their Nipperkins at the Tavern" decided that strong action should be taken. They persuaded the landlord to enter the room and snuff the candles by pouring sulphur over them.

Ned Ward reported :

When the lights fizzled out and there was an evil smelling darkness, one of the merry God-fearing Gentlemen covered himself in a bearskin and came into the room crying in a deep voice, "I'm the devil come to take one of you." But for a few who were too drunk to move, the sceptic circle disassembled and did not meet again at Cripplegate.

It seems more than likely that the great John Wilkes, "the defender of liberty," had read Ned Ward, since he brought about the end of "The Hell-Fire Club" in a similar way. While they were celebrating the Black Mass and Lord Orford was offering up a prayer to Satan, Wilkes released into the room a large baboon dressed as the devil. The "monks" and the "nuns" believing that their prayer had been answered fled in confusion and never met again. Did Wilkes, who was not in favour then with Sir Francis Dashwood, get this idea from Ned Ward? Who knows? One thing, however, is certain. "The Atheistical Club" at Cripplegate was a pale imitation of the great "Hell-Fire Club" at Medmenham. Ned Ward was ahead of his time in another way. He was the first writer to describe prostitutes as "nuns" and to give the mistress of a brothel the honorary title of "the abbess." The most eminent of these ladies was Charlotte Hayes, who has been sanctified in the annals of bawdry as "Santa Carlotta."

9

THE NUN'S STORY

> While womanhood in habit of a nun,
> At Mednam lies by backwood monks undone.

The Reverend Charles Churchill, poet, rake and Anglican parson, who wrote those lines had some experience of the nuns of Medmenham, which they will tell you in that part of Buckinghamshire is pronounced Mednam. Although he was a junior member of the order, the Reverend Churchill had for some time a particular interest in what was the most licentious gathering of men and women who ever met to enjoy themselves on English soil. In their bawdiness, they excelled all the libertines of the reign of Charles II. Not even the great Chevalier Casanova, who was madly pursuing women in England at the same time, was their equal. The story of the Medmenham monks is certainly the most remarkable in the history of Buckinghamshire. The analist of that county, George Liscombe, wrote :

> The less creditable events in the shire were the scenes of debauchery performed at Medmenham Abbey near the Thames.

Performance is the right word. The settings were as elaborate as any ever designed for a mammoth stage production. The interior of the Abbey was elegantly furnished. In the rooms and corridors soft lights burned behind rose coloured windows. At night, tiny lanterns were suspended from trees in the gardens where the nuns strolled with their amorous monks.

He tells us that each monk was allowed to bring with him "a lady of a cheerful and lively disposition, who embraces a general hilarity." Cheerful, lively and hilarious these nuns most certainly were. In the early days of the order, they were the wives of local squires. While in the monastery they belonged body and soul to the members of the order. Everything was carried out according to strict rules. The author of *Nocturnal Revels* gave some details of the procedure :

> No lady may be taken by surprise. They are admitted in masks and do not unmask till all the brethren have passed them in review. They may retire without apology or revealing themselves to any but their temporary husbands.

There were many secluded places out of doors where the rites of Venus could be celebrated. If they felt so disposed each monk and his nun could row along the Thames in one of the many boats supplied by the ever thoughtful Sir Francis. We have this charming account of other forms of recreation :

> Disquisitions of an amorous kind are introduced, in which full liberty of speech is allowed, within the prescribed limits of decorum.

We are not told what these limits were but it would seem likely that there was very little restraint about praise of the female form or declarations of love. The account continues :

> In case the topic should unexpectedly become too warm or passionate, the use of fans is allowed to prevent the appearance of the Ladies' blushes : and under these circumstances, some women seize the opportunity for a temporary retreat with their paramours.

Scarcely any convenience had been overlooked :

> The Monastery is not destitute of the aid of the obstetric art : as the Ladies in case they find it necessary may want to absent themselves from the World and assist posterity with respect to the rising generation.

Midwifery on a large scale may not have been necessary but the medicine man among the monks could always be otherwise occupied, supplying love potions to all who wished to have them. Girlish laughter came from a recreation room where the nuns could play games among themselves or ride on a large rocking hobby-horse if they felt particularly frolicsome.

It may be wondered what the squires of the district thought about these diversions of their wives. All we can assume is that the country gentlemen in this part of Buckinghamshire were more trustful than most husbands are today. The time came, however, when the squires began to enquire why their wives were spending so much time away from home. The news about the goings-on in the woods and shady nooks by the riverside had been observed by many of the villagers. The upshot was that the husbands flatly refused to allow their wives to go a roving any more with the monks. This was a severe blow to "The Order of St. Francis." They were obliged to look elsewhere for nuns. It is on record that there were no female servants at the Abbey and country wenches, even if willing, would not have had the aplomb or expertise of the squires' wives.

There was only one thing to do. Since there was no longer a supply of amateurs, they must engage professionals. Sir Francis Dashwood, the founder of the order, who was Chancellor of the Exchequer in the British Government, had a sideline as a shareholder in the brothel run by "Mother" Stanhope at Covent Garden. He knew that she would be only too glad to help the monks out of their difficulty. Most of the members knew other sources of supply. They put their heads together. In the end, the new idea was a success.

It so happened that the Earl of Sandwich, First Lord of the Admiralty, was on most friendly terms with Catherine Hayes, who kept "A Parlour for the Aristocracy" at King Street near Drury Lane. There were, of course, several similar establishments. Moll King was mistress of a well-run house near Temple Bar and Mrs. Goadby had a very select brothel in Berwick Street, Soho. Both were well known to members of the fraternity, to Lord Melcombe Regis, for example, M.P. for Middlesex and Treasurer of the Navy, to Thomas Potter, the Paymaster-General and secretary to the Prince of Wales, and to Paul Whitehead, High Steward of the order.

There was the Hon. Jack Spencer, grandson of the Duchess of Marlborough and the Reverend Charles Churchill, both of whom knew where the best Covent Garden Ladies could be found. At the heels of the hunt, the main contract went to Charlotte Hayes.

After Sir Francis, the most important monk was the First Lord of the Admiralty, the Earl of Sandwich. He had bestowed on Catherine the title of "Santa Carlotta." She fully warranted this sanctification. Sandwich, you will know, was so busy at his office at Whitehall that he could find time only during working hours and while playing cards to eat large chunks of meat between slices of bread, thus giving to a snack a name which has lasted ever since. Because of his cabinet rank, the Sandwich Islands were also called after him. He had no trouble persuading his colleagues that in Santa Carlotta he had made a wise choice. "She has always," he said, "a good stock of virgins in store. She supplies the Stock Exchange with real immaculate maidenheads." This was a high recommendation and an undeniable truth.

The author of *Satan's Harvest Home*, published anonymously in 1749, recorded that Mrs. Hayes "made her daily rounds of the city to see what youth or beauty the country had sent to London." When she was lucky enough to find "a pretty, fresh rural girl," she dressed her up in the latest fashion and called her "a milliner's assistant" or "a parson's daughter," two titles which seem to have had an appeal to the rakes of the period. If she happened to meet a regular customer on her rounds, Santa Carlotta would tell him about the new girls who had joined her *bagnio* and suggest that he might like to drop in and have a look round.

There were at that time some twenty good houses of pleasure in the centre of London, the best of them patronised by aldermen, Members of Parliament and the nobility. Generally speaking they were well-run establishments. In the case of Santa Carlotta, it was a matter of dealing with an old-established firm, almost, you might say, carrying on business by royal appointment. Frederick, Prince of Wales, a member of "The Order of St Francis," was not a stranger there, nor was his friend, the Prime Minister, the Earl of Bute, as canny a Scots lad as ever wore a sporran. He was at Egham races one day when a heavy shower of rain began to fall. The Prince of Wales who was also having a flutter that day invited Bute, whom he didn't then know, to his tent to make a fourth at a game of whist. The Prince—his father, George II, called him "the booby," took a fancy to the young Scot and made him "A Gentleman to his Bedchamber." Bute was no sooner installed than he became the lover of the Princess of Wales, Augusta. Before long he was Prime Minister of England. That's how many things were done in those Georgian days. Both the Prince and the Prime Minister would have approved of Santa Carlotta as London agent for the order. So would George Selwyn, M.P. for Gloucester, a wit who loved watching executions and was one of Santa Carlotta's best customers. She sent him this invitation card:

> Mrs. Hayes presents her most respected compliments and wishes to say that tomorrow evening at 7 p.m., Twelve Beautiful Nymphs, unsullied and untainted, will perform the celebrated rites of Venus as practised by Otaheite under the instructions of Queen Oborea, in which character Mrs. Hayes will appear on this occasion.

So important was Santa Carlotta that, if it had been asked to approve, the British Cabinet would have ratified her appointment. She conducted her house on sound business lines, as may be seen from items in her diary.

> Jan. 9. A maid for Alderman —. Nell Blossom, nineteen, has not been in company for four days.

> Colonel —. A modest girl, Mrs. Mitchell's cook, just come from the country and a new face. The Countess le Fleur from Seven Dials.

> Dr. —. After church is over.

Santa Carlotta punctiliously fulfilled her commitments. She had an important commission for June 18, 1759.

> Twelve nuns for the Abbey. Something discreet and Cyprian for the Friars.

Eastern methods of making love had grown popular in London, mainly in the Divan Club at the Thatched Tavern in St. James's Street. The members there made themselves up to look like Turks and carried daggers. The ladies wore silken bloomers and hid their faces with yashmaks.

> The Divan wantons little scruple shows,
> They hide their faces and their bums expose.

Those lines come from a lampoon aimed at Philip, Duke of Wharton, founder of the Divan Club. It continued :

> When Molly How shall dare become a saint,
> And Nancy cease to wear such loads of paint,
> When Biddy Knowle's maidenhead is found,
> And Sally Maples once again is sound.
> When Wharton's just and learns to pay his debts,
> And Reputation dwells at Madame Brett's.
> When Ministers of State dry up their sores,
> And one by one disband their troop of whores.

But let us go back to Santa Carlotta making her plans for this June day in 1759. It was not such an easy job to find twelve girls who would satisfy all the desires of the friars. As well as good looks some decorum was essential. This was not always a quality to be found even in the most exclusive brothels. It was like finding the best actresses for a royal command production of a play with an all-women cast. With her friend, Betty Wymes, the belle of the Rose Tavern in Drury Lane, Charlotte began to make a list of possible starters. There was Betty herself, already well known to the monks. There was Elizabeth Roach, one of Dashwood's favourite girls, there was Kitty Fisher who was described as "the most pretty, extravagant, wicked little whore who ever flourished," there was beautiful Lucy Cooper, who would dance naked to "Here we go round the Mulberry Bush," and there was Betsy Carless, "the most handsome woman around Covent Garden." There was Fanny Murray, the most sought-after London courtesan at that time in London. Some of these ladies were in permanant employment and might not want to leave London.

If the records of "The Order of St. Francis" had not been destroyed, we would know more about the identity of the nuns and their part in the orgies at West Wycombe. We can only assume that when Santa Carlotta had made her selection, the twelve happy girls sailed down the Thames in a hired barge to Marlow, looking forward to the time of their lives. They would sing and chatter gaily as if they were going on an excursion from a convent school. There was no rivalry or cattiness, just *eprit de corps*. It was like when Peg Woffington said to one of her close friends, "You must have Manners, dear." She was not talking about politeness but referring to one of her own admirers, John Manners, Marquis of Granby, and suggesting that she would arrange an assignment with him for her friend. The party on its way to Medmenham would be as excited as the young ladies from the brothel of Madame Tellier when she took them for a day's outing in the story by de Maupassant.

When they reached Marlow, the girls would be escorted to the Abbey. They would take off their gay summer clothes and dress in the simple habits provided by the monks. The initial ceremony would then begin. As head of the order, Sir Francis would wear a scarlet robe and a large red biretta. The other monks were dressed in white. The proceedings would open with a celebration of the Black Mass. The monks, let it be said, were staunch Protestants and liked to mock the Roman Catholic faith.

When the ritual had been observed, the revels began. The nuns could walk in the gardens which were laid out in the shape of a naked woman. Here and there were statues of male figures in poses that might encourage amorous desires. For the delectation of the men, there was a naked Venus stooping to pick a thorn from her foot. This was a favourite with Lord Melcombe-Regis, Lord of the Treasury and M.P. for Winchelsea. "If he goes on," said Wilkes, "as he has since the monks came here, he will die in harness to some woman who can stay the pace better than a paunchy old sexagerarian like him." Lord Melcombe-Regis was the Friar Tuck of the order and a constant source of amusement to the brothers and the nuns. When he fell asleep in an easy chair, one of the lively young women would steal out to the vegetable garden and bring in a large carrot and two small turnips to place between his legs.

Before dinner some of the monks and nuns would sail down the river in a great red gondola which Sir Francis had brought from Venice. Food and drink were plentiful. A favourite dish, "The Breasts of Venus," consisted of the white flesh of chickens with a single red cherry on the top of each. In bowls everywhere there were the most luscious fruit and sweetmeats. The drinks served had such evocative names as "Strip me Naked" and "Lay me Down Softly." In references to the revels we read of "strange foods and wine being poured by naked girls in the drinking chambers of the Chapter House."

So much has been written contradictory about "The Order of St. Francis" that it is difficult to reach the kernel of the truth. We know that the inner circle consisted only of twelve members. That was why Santa Carlotta was asked to provide no more than that number of nuns. But although the dozen brothers were the mainstay of the fraternity, their close friends could always find accommodation and entertainment there. Frederick, Prince of Wales, was on the list of visitors, so was Henry Fox, Lord Holland, "Old Q," the famous Earl of March, Lawrence Sterne, the novelist, and Edmund Duffield, the Vicar of Medmenham. If the Prime Minister, the Earl of Bute, wanted to get away from the Princess of Wales and the strain of office, he could bring one or other of his mistresses to the Abbey for a quiet weekend. When he came to London, Benjamin Franklin, "the greatest American of his time," found Sir Francis Dashwood a genial host. "I am in this house," wrote Franklin, "as much at my ease as if it were my own."

Franklin and Dashwood were most certainly birds of a feather. The American statesman, philosopher and author, was a confirmed rake. He was no stranger to the brothels of Philadelphia where, we are told, "he spent much time in bawdiness, revelry and drinking rum." Franklin was a rum bird in every way. Like so many men of talent, he was fond of strong drink and women. Now and then he burst into amorous verse :

> Fair Venus calls, her voice obey,
> In Beauty's arms spend night and day,
> The joys of love all joys excel,
> And loving's certainly doing well.

As a journalist and proprietor of *The Philadelphia*

Gazette, Franklin would enjoy one of Dashwood's ways of amusing his guests. He would take a newspaper, transpose certain lines and produce sentences like these:

> This morning the Speaker of the House of Commons
> Was convicted of keeping a disorderly house.

> Tonight His Majesty will go in State
> To fifteen notorious prostitutes

Time for the nuns, the monks and guests passed pleasantly at Medmenham. When they could meet such men of power and influence as Prime Minister Bute, the Prince of Wales or Benjamin Franklin, it was exciting for the young women from the nunnery of Santa Carlotta to be invited to the Abbey. We can only guess at their names. The brothers were sworn to secrecy about the identity of all their nuns and the girls in turn were expected to keep quiet about the men they met there. Lady Betty Germain was a regular visitor to the Abbey but she was an amateur and not dependent on prostitution for a living. She knew Casanova when he spent some years in London. The extraordinary thing is that Chevalier Casanova never got to Medmenham, though he knew Fanny Murray, Kitty Fisher and others who were on the books of Jack Harris and Santa Carlotta. All the words in English Casanova knew were "I love you," but even with this disadvantage he managed to get by in London.

But if Casanova never found his way to Medmenham, another Chevalier from the continent did. We shall never know exactly what part Chevalier D'Eon de Beaumont played at the Medmenham orgies. In his book, *The Hell-Fire Club,* Donald McCormick gives a list of the girls, amateur and professional, who can be assumed to have been selected as nuns. Among the ladies, he places the Chevalier D'Eon de Beaumont, whose sex was a matter of speculation for a long time. He was undoubtedly a "Mollie" but what one inclined that way was doing amid all the masculinity of the monks is a mystery. On May 24, 1771, the Chevalier was examined of his own free will by a number of ladies who could only express the opinion that they were in doubt about whether he was a man or a woman. All gambling men, the monks made large wagers among themselves on this most controversial subject. It seems that more than a thousand pounds worth of bets were laid. Still no clear-cut decision could be reached. It was not, in fact, till 1777 that another examination took place in connection with the Chevalier's fortune. The jury decided that he was female. From then on, the Chevalier spent the rest of his life in women's clothes. When he died, the doctors declared definitely that he was a man.

We have no evidence what kind of garb the Chevalier wore when he was at Medmenham. The likely thing is that both the monks and the nuns treated him as a joke, as they did Horace Walpole.

It was be that D'Eon like Walpole was merely an observer. For this kind of visitor, Sir Francis had also made provision. On the top of the church at West Wycombe he had erected a large golden ball where ten people could sit and admire the gardens and the surrounding countryside. There was, however, one part of the abbey which no visitor, no matter how distinguished, was permitted to enter. The Chapter Room was the sanctum sanctorum. Even Wilkes, after he was expelled from the order, had little to say about what went on in that holy place. We can only assume that there the nuns paraded naked for the important orgiastic and fertility rites. Charles Johnston in a tedious book, *Chrysal*, published in 1785, reported that "the monks and the nuns would vie with each other in much lewdness."

The whole proceedings were like dreams come true of what the monks would have desired a sexual paradise to be. In his book about the Georgian rakes, Aubrey Jones has this to say about Dashwood and his friends :

> It may have been an immoral dream but it was also a good-natured and extremely sociable one. Their motto was "Love and Friendship." It was their misfortune that their loves came from the brothels and that their friendships were badly cracked on the rock of politics.

The Medmenhamites took as a pattern the Abbey of Theleme, as described by Rabelais. There were no clocks there in case the monks should waste time counting the hours. Only the most beautiful women were admitted.

There is still a certain amount of mystery surrounding the identities of the ladies who gave their favours to the monks. According to a prominent member of the order, John Wilkes, Lord Mayor of London and M.P. for Aylesbury, the frolics went on not only indoors but in "the gardens, the groves and the adjoining woods." This would explain the use of the word "backwood" in Churchill's verse. The monks on summer evenings and moonlit nights strolled with their nuns through a kind of fairyland. Each one had his cell indoors where he was sure of being alone with the lady of his choice. Leigh Hunt hit the right note when he wrote :

> If you become a nun, dear,
> A friar I will be,
> To any cell you run, dear,
> Pray, look around for me.

The nuns had no reason to run to their cells. They went happily hand in hand with the friars along the corridors or were playfully carried there. Beneath their habits, they were naked, to make disrobing only a matter of a second.

For first-hand information about Medmenham, we must go to *Nocturnal Revels*, a book published anonymously in 1778 by a man who described himself as "A Monk of the Order of St. Francis." He may have belonged to the inner circle or have been initiated as a guest.

If we judge by the portraits of some of the courtesans who were nuns as West Wycombe, they fulfilled the requirements of the French Abbey of Theleme. Most of them were beautiful and young. Wilkes called them "little satin bottoms." The majority of the monks were by no means handsome. Sandwich was an unusually ugly man, Lord Melcombe-Regis was grossly fat and repulsive. Paul Whitehead, the Steward, was old and decrepit. Wilkes had charm with an unprepossessing appearance. The most virile was Dashwood, who had a rugged masculinity, an impish smile and a dignity that must have had a strong appeal for women.

The revels at Medmenham usually took place in the summer and went on for a week. Then, wrote Johnston, who was an Irish Catholic and disliked the blasphemy of the order, "the slaves of their lust went back to the brothels whence they had been brought." In *Chrysal*, there is a full account of "The Order of St. Francis." The "Master," to whom Chrysal, the story-teller, refers may have been Wilkes. Some writers think he was the Reverend Charles Churchill. Johnston must have read Ned Ward's account of the final meeting of "The Aethiestical Club" in London. How else could he have described a similar happening at West Wycombe?

> My Master contrived the night before to bring into his cell a great baboon. He dressed the creature up in which childish imagination clothes devils.

When he got his opportunity, Chrysal's master shut the monkey up in a large chest in the Chapter room.

> To the spring of the lock of the chest my Master fastened a cord which he drew under the carpet on the floor of his own seat and brought the end of it through a hole which he had made in such a manner that he could easily find it: and by giving it a pull let the baboon out whenever he pleased. Accordingly when the monks were invoking Satan, my Master pulled the cord. The baboon, glad to be released from his confinement, gave a sudden spring on to the middle of the table.
>
> Terrified out of their senses, the monks roared as of in one voice, "The Devil, the Devil," and started for the door, tumbling over each other and upsetting everything in their way.

Whether this joke was perpetrated by John Wilkes or the Reverend Charles Churchill is a matter of indifference. It is a good story but it doesn't ring true. The final information available about "The Hell-Fire Club" and "The Order of St. Francis" appeared in *The Morning Post* on August 22, 1776.

> The Order of the Francisan Society of Medmenham Abbey being nearly demolished, Jemmy Twicher, who is almost the only surviving member of that club, is determined to restore it to its original glory.

The Morning Post had been told that new members were to be initiated into "this infernal society." But they were misinformed. "The Hell-Fire Club" was well and truly

dead. Not even Jemmy Twicher could bring it back to life.
Nobody in London ever thought of giving Sandwich his
proper title. He had been given the name "Jemmy
Twicher" from a character in *The Beggar's Opera*. But that
is another story. One of the most popular pamphlets on
sale in London was the scurrilous *Life Adventures, Intrigues
and Amours of the celebrated Jemmy Twicher.*

Even this publicity did not discourage the first Lord of
the Admiralty, who was the greatest rake of all his colleagues in the British Cabinet. There is little doubt that one
of his many mistresses, Fanny Murray, was also one of the
Medmenham nuns. As a girl she had been seduced by
another member of the order, the Hon. Jack Spencer, who
had inherited all the good qualities and some of the vices
of the Marlborough family. When he deserted her in Bath,
she went to London and was taken under the wings of both
Santa Carlotta and Moll King, who was a sub-contractor
for the supply of nuns for the friars. When the girls returned to these two ladies in London, they would have
happy memories of the amorous dallyings in the gardens
and woods and the nights of lovemaking in the cells. They
would laugh heartily about the sight of Lord Melcombe-
Regis decorated from the vegetable garden as he lay asleep.
They would recall the boisterous ribaldry of Dashwood and
Sandwich, the rich food and exotic drinks. The Reverend
Charles Churchill, who looked like a prizefighter and was
both a good poet and philosopher, would have amused
them by reciting bawdy verse in praise of Venus :

> The grasp divine, the emphatic, thrilling squeeze,
> The throbbing, panting breasts, the trembling knees,
> The tickling motion, the enlivening flow,
> The rapturous shiver and dissolving—Oh.

In a less erotic vein, Churchill wrote verse that went
much deeper :

> When satire flies abroad on falsehood's wing,
> Short is her life and impotent her sting.
> But when to truth allied, the wound she gives
> Sinks deep and to remotest ages lives.

No body of men have ever been greater targets for satire

than the members of "The Order of St. Francis" and the "Hell-Fire Club." Many falsehoods may have been written about them but also many truths. We know more about them than we do about their women. We can only guess about the names of the nuns and the parts they played at Medmenham. There is, however, plenty of information about their lives in London. The stories of Fanny Murray, Nancy Parsons, Kitty Fisher and other courtesans are part of the history of the Georgian years. So, of course, are the activities of the monks when they were not in residence at the Abbey.

10

WILKES AND LIBERTY

The harlots cry from street to street,
Shall weave old England's winding sheet.

That prophecy by William Blake may have been suggested
by the profligacy of the men with power and influence who
governed Britain for so many years. But it was not true of
the past nor is it likely to be fulfilled in the future. Harlots
of one kind or another have played their parts in the lives
of many great men. So has a fondness for strong drink.
Wine and women may have brought ruin to some men but
to more they have been almost a blessing and a necessity.
John Wilkes is a perfect example. All his setbacks—and
he had quite a few—were not due to his endless pursuit of
women or excessive intemperance but to his independent
spirit and a pen that was both obscene and at times vicious.

He was the most talented member of "The Order of St.
Francis" and "The Hell-Fire Club." He was richly endowed
with a sense of humour and a ready wit, even as a child.
When his father, a wealthy distiller in Clerkenwell, asked
him jokingly if he had a purse, he answered "No." Then he
pointed out that money was the first requisite, since without
that you couldn't buy a purse. First things always came first
to John Wilkes. To him a high priority was the company
of attractive and lustful women.

It was evident that he would make a name for himself
in the England of those Georgian days, as a writer, a politician, a wit and a most accomplished rake. The story has
often been told of his reply to his one-time friend and later
sworn enemy, the Earl of Sandwich, who told him that he
would "die either of a pox or on the scaffold." "That
depends," said Wilkes, "on whether I embrace your prin-
ciples or your mistress. He was equally ready for a heckler

when he was candidate for the seat in Parliament he won at Aylesbury. A man called out "I'd rather vote for the devil than for you." "And what would you do," Wilkes asked, "if your friend wasn't standing?"

John Wilkes began his long record of rakery when he was a student at Leyden University. In London later, under the expert guidance of his friend, Thomas Potter, he became a habitué of the best brothels. It was Potter, a barrister and son of the Archbishop of Canterbury, who introduced him to the "Hell-Fire Club." The Archbishop had generously given his son a hundred thousand pounds which he and Wilkes began to spend on riotous living. There was scarcely a town within fifty miles of London where Potter didn't know a wench. "I poison all my friends' morals," he said. The wife of the Bishop of Gloucester fell for his charm and gave him a son. He had girl friends everywhere. "If you meet Miss Betty Spooner," he wrote to Wilkes, "offer incense to her for my sake. You will find her all liveliness and lecherous."

No matter where Wilkes went there was always a Betty Spooner, a Kitty Towler or a Lucy Ballard, two of his early girl friends in London. There was a very attractive Mrs. Gardner, on whom he could always call. If he wished to spend an evening at home, there was his equally delightful housekeeper, Catherine Smith, who bore him a son. Most important of all on his list was a most luscious woman of thirty, whom Casanova had tried in vain to win during his stay in London. Both her mother and her grandmother had been courtesans in Paris and in Berne. In her younger days, the grandmother had been forced to earn her living as a common streetwalker. This was also the misfortune of her three illegitimate daughters. Genevieve, the grand-daughter, was the first to make a real success of the profession. A shapely girl, with a mass of dark brown hair, she was only a short time in London till she became one of the most sought-after Covent Garden ladies. As was the case with John Wilkes in his letter from Potter, Casanova arrived in England with a letter of introduction from a friend to Genevieve, "the most desirable whore in London." But the great lover, maybe for the first time in his life, was out of luck. Genevieve de Charpillon had just become the favourite mistress of John Wilkes, then Lord Mayor of London. The Chevalier Casanova saw her and pleaded with her in vain.

Wilkes first set eyes on her at the Swan Inn in Chelsea and immediately decided that she would be the new woman in his life. She had charm, grace, a lovely piquant face and she spoke endearingly in a broken English which intrigued him. No woman knew better how to please a man than Mademoiselle de Charpillon, a name she had taken when the Swiss government had deported the entire family from Berne. In coming to London instead of some other capital city, they had made a happy choice. In Switzerland and in France, Genevieve's customers had been mostly men of the working class. Now she had captured the Lord Mayor of London. The family—the original name was Bruner—were living at this time in Soho. Wilkes, though heavily in debt, was so enamoured that he provided them with a better house in Great Titchfield Street.

The fun and games with the nuns at Medmenham were now only a memory. No more wenching in the woods or copulation in a cell for the most popular politican in the whole of Britain. He was now over fifty. He had still plenty of virility but he was beginning to find Genevieve too demanding and possessive. If he didn't call every day, she would write him illiterate notes in French, since she was able only to say a few words of endearment in English. Their liaison, nevertheless, lasted four years. When they parted on good terms, Wilkes took a careful note of her new address in case he might have a sudden urge to see her again.

He had as it happened found another mistress, a quiet country girl, Amelia Arnold. He set her up in a delightful house in Kensington Gore, where they lived openly together. She was a domesticated woman who could cook good dinners for his friends. He was so fond of her that he took her for a holiday with him to the Isle of Wight. In the course of time, she bore him a daughter, who became one of the great comforts of his old age. One of his great virtues was a love for children, whether they were his own or belonged to somebody else. His portraits show him as a kindly, thoughtful man, by no means handsome. If you look at his figure in Chelsea porcelain at the British Museum, you will see him as a tall, slender man, dressed in knee breeches and an elaborate coat. Beneath him appropriately is a small cherubic Cupid. Wearing a cocked hat and scarlet cloak, he would walk all the way from the Guildhall to Amelia's house at Kensington Gore in all kinds of weather, ignoring the coachmen who recognised him, touched their hats and asked if he wanted a cab.

Although she was his most constant companion at the time, Amelia was not the only one. On a visit to Bath, he met and fell in love with beautiful Mrs. Stafford who had been deserted by her "puppy of a husband," as great a libertine as Wilkes himself. So there he was with Mrs. Stafford in Bath and Amelia at Kensington Gore.

On his list at the same time was a lively young wanton, Jenny Wade, whom he had met in a tavern near Fleet Street. As well as brothels, there were in London a number of discreet private hotels where men of high position could meet their mistresses. A favourite one of these was run by a genteel lady, Mrs. Muilman, off the Strand. Mrs. Nelson had a similar rendezvous in Wardour Street. When he was not in Bath or Kensington, Wilkes found it convenient to meet Polly at one or other of these hide-outs instead of setting her up in a house which she was constantly urging him to do. She was an extravagent young woman, this pretty Polly and "St. John of Aylesbury," his sanctified title when he was a monk at West Wycombe, found her lively and amusing. His lovemaking was becoming too expensive and he was unable to afford another home. In earlier times he would certainly have taken Polly down to Medmenham for the frolics there. She was the kind of girl who would have thoroughly enjoyed herself among the monks.

There has always been some doubt about the real reason for the expulsion of John Wilkes from "The Order of St. Francis." Some believe that it was because he was the culprit in the release of the baboon. But that would not appear to be so from what we know from Charles Johnston in *Chrysal*. More likely the fact is that he disliked intensely some of his brother monks, especially Prime Minister Bute and Melcombe-Regis, Lord of the Treasury.

The real trouble seems to have arisen when Wilkes took exception to the Earl of Bute being made a member of "The Order of St. Francis." Whatever these men may have had in common in the Abbey, they were at daggers drawn in the world of politics. One of the other monks had called brother Prime Minister "Brutish Bute, the Scots hanzie with a false heart." They were clearly not all one big happy family at Medmenham. Wilkes said that Dashwood had been appointed Chancellor of the Exchequer because of long experience and skill "at reckoning up tavern bills." Bute had become Prime Minister at the same time because the Princess Augusta, wife of Frederick Louis, Prince of Wales, had accepted him as her lover after her husband had made him "Gentleman of the Bedchamber."

Frederick Louis was the most likeable of all the Georgian princes. Doubt had been cast on whether or not he was the son of George II. The scandal-mongers at court spread the rumour when they looked at his sallow complexion that maybe one or other of the Turkish valets, Mustapha or Mahomet, might have been connected with his birth. As a young man, Frederick Louis was as rakish as any of the Hanoverians. One of the royal pages wrote to his brother to say that in St. James's Park "the Prince was robbed of his watch, twenty-two guineas and a gold medal by a girl." When a grenadier offered to try to find the strumpet, Frederick told him that all he wanted back was the watch and that "she was welcome to the money."

Another indiscretion of Frederick's young manhood was to buy for £1,500 "the daughter of a hautboy player" in the theatre. His evil genius was Lord Hervey, a courtier, who had an attractive mistress, Vanelle Vane, a small and pretty little doll, known in Court circles as "The Dwarf." To gain influence over the Prince Hervey made him a present of Miss Vane. In due time a son was born at her home in Soho and christened Fitz-Frederick Vane. Nobody ever knew whether the boy belonged to Hervey or the Prince. If Frederick Louis was the father then young Master Vane would have been the elder brother of the future

George III and might well have claimed the throne. But that was not to happen.

Next to Hervey in the corruption of Frederick Louis came John Stuart, third Earl of Bute, whose hobby was amateur acting. A handsome and extremely pompous man, he appealed to the Princess Augusta, herself a stately beauty, on their first meeting. Everybody but the Prince seemed to know that the woman who was looking forward to being Queen of England and his friend, Bute, were lovers. The ever watchful gossip writer, Horace Walpole, was "as much convinced of an amorous connection between Lord Bute and the Princess" as if he had seen them in bed together. It was noticed by another writer that "Lord Bute enjoys a higher place in the favour of the Princess than is compatible with strict propriety."

In his biography of Frederick Louis, Sir Charles Young has this to say about the sudden death of the Prince.

> Did the Princess poison him? It is not impossible. She has never been accused of it: but there is a case to be made against her.

After the death of Frederick Louis, Bute used to visit Augusta hidden in the curtain chair of one of her ladies-in-waiting. A clever woman, the Princess Augusta persuaded her father-in-law, the now ageing George II, to make her lover his chief adviser. You will remember that George was "the comedian king" who told lavatorial jokes and died appropriately on one of the new water closets installed at Kensington Palace. When this sad event had taken place and her son, George III became king, Augusta got Bute made Prime Minister, with a special commission to launch a campaign against the Whigs, the most dangerous of them being John Wilkes, the "St. John of Aylesbury" at the Abbey. He was constantly attacking the Bute administration in *The North Briton*.

It was not, however, politics but sex that made the monks fall out among each other. Wilkes printed his obscene poem, "Essay on Woman," a copy of which is preserved in the Dyce Library at the Victoria and Albert Museum. The original version began with the words "Arise my Fanny" and went on at considerable length with many lines that are unprintable.

Everybody knew that Fanny Murray had been the mistress of Sandwich. The most vicious rake of all, he didn't care a tinker's curse if all London knew about his private life away from his Cabinet post. What he saw was an opportunity to bring about the downfall of Wilkes and improve his own position among the Tories. Whether Wilkes wrote all the "Essay on Woman" or if his friend, Potter, was co-author is as great a matter of doubt as whether Shakespeare or Bacon wrote the plays. Wilkes, however, was forced to take the rap. It came about like this. Although it was set up in type, the "Essay" was not printed to be read by everybody. It was, perhaps, intended more as a private joke among a chosen few.

It so happened that one of the most dissolute rakes of the period, the Earl of March, "Old 'Q'," had a chaplain, the Reverend John Kidgell, rector of Horne in Surrey. This most suitable father-confessor to "Old 'Q' " was a collector of all the pornographic works that could be found and was himself the author of an obscene novel, *The Card*. Among the licentious clergy of the day, Kidgell was the chief. From a printer, he got a copy of the "Essay," showed it his master, who thoroughly enjoyed its ribaldry. He sent the work to Sandwich. By this time there was no brotherly love between him and Wilkes. Off his own bat, Sandwich took immediate action and brought about one of the big sensations of the day. No such vulgarity or filth had ever before polluted the distinguished chamber of the House of Lords.

Sandwich was as proud of his lasciviousness as he was of his profanity. He kept a baboon, maybe the same one that created the trouble at the Abbey. A bishop whom he was entertaining to dinner one evening, asked if he might say grace. Sandwich made an excuse to leave the room, returned a moment later with the baboon and ordered it to make the prayer. Shocked but composed, the bishop said quietly, "I wasn't aware that you had a brother in holy orders." As he had tried to offend the bishop, so did he decide to provoke the more sedate members of the House of Lords. When unexpectedly he arose and began to read the most disgraceful passages to the assembled peers, several of them demanded that he should stop. He continued to the bitter end, reading lines that would have almost made a back-street harlot blush. He found an ally in Bishop Warburton, whose wife Potter had seduced and who had also been mentioned in the "Essay." The bishop told the Lords that in his opinion Wilkes was one of the "fiends of Hell," then made the apology, "I injure these elder sons of perdition by this comparison." When all opinions had been expressed, the House of Lords decided that John Wilkes had been "guilty of writing and publishing a most scandalous, obscene and impious libel." The House of Commons later endorsed this opinion.

Sandwich revelled in his triumph. When he spoke some days later at the Beefstake Club, several actors, men who are not easily annoyed by strong language, left the table and the tavern in disgust.

Sandwich was expelled from the Beefsteak Club for his blasphemy and foul language. Wilkes was expelled from the House of Commons for having written his "Essay on Woman." He at once shook the dust of England off his heels and went to Paris. He was only a short time there when he met the most beautiful woman he had ever known. Her name was Gertrude Maria Corradini, an Italian and an unsuccessful dancer who had become a courtesan. Wilkes first saw her at the house of a friend and was completely captivated. "She was a perfect Grecian figure," he wrote in his later years, "cast in the mould of the Florentine Venus, except that she was rather taller." This affair lasted twelve months and had an unhappy ending. When she went back to her native city of Bologna, Wilkes immediately followed her. In the belief that his money was running down, she packed up every valuable piece of goods in the villa where they were staying and did a moonlit flit. He never saw her again and never forgave her, but he had another string to his bow. While the affair with la Corradini was at its height, he had been living in a flat in the Rue de Saint Peres, where the attractive landlady was Madame Chassagne, a discarded mistress of the ballet master at the Opera House. It was like "Tam O'Shanter" in the poem by Rabbie Burns :

> The landlady and Tam grew gracious,
> With favours sweet and very gracious.

But, alas, Madame Chassagne had much the same idea as La Corradini. Short of cash herself, she got her hands on all the money Wilkes had in his room and disappeared one morning early. He was annoyed but not vanquished. There was always another woman. He took under his wing a pretty little prostitute, Louise Dufort, and was perfectly happy with her for a time. He wrote to his friend, the Reverend Churchill :

> I long to introduce you here to the prettiest little bubbies and the most pouting lips I have ever kissed.

He was now almost down to his last ha'penny but good fortune lay ahead. By this time the climate of politics had changed in England. One of his friends, the Duke of Grafton, was now Prime Minister and the envy of all admirers of women for the fact that his mistress was Nancy Parsons, the most stately and beautiful of all London courtesans, as can be seen in her portrait by Gainsborough. Grafton responded cordially to a letter from Wilkes and offered him a post. With some bitter sweet memories, he returned home. Before long the *St. James's Chronicle* was reporting :

> Saturday last, the Rt. Hon. the Marquis of Grafton, John Wilkes, Esq., and the Rev. Mr. C. Churchill, seated themselves in the same Box at Drury Lane Theatre, and received on the Occasion such loud Shouts of Applause from the Spectators, as for some Time interrupted the Performance.

The capital letters were justified. The banished rebel was soon to become the most popular politician in England. It was almost like what Ned Ward called the story of "Whittington-Cat."

At the top of the poll he was elected M.P. for the County of Middlesex. He became an alderman, High Sheriff and Lord Mayor of London. He was High Chamberlain when the freedom of the city was conferred on Sir Horatio Nelson after his great victory at the Battle of Cape

St. Vincent. The man who had for a time been imprisoned in the Tower, who had shamefully deserted his wife, who was the greatest libertine of his time in England, was honoured by the greatest of the land. The society hostesses who had once ignored him now opened wide their doors to him. In his declining years, he was comforted by his legal daughter, Polly, and the illegitimate girl born to Amelia Arnold. Both adored him and he was devoted to them. On his seventieth birthday, he told them with a twinkle in his eye, "I must be 140 today. I have always packed the life of two days into one."

The cry, "Wilkes and Liberty" greeted him everywhere he went. At a military review, a young soldier asked a drummer who "the queer-looking old chap with the bald head was?" "That's Johnny Wilkes," was the reply, "and that bald head has more brains in it than all our regiments put together—and that includes the drummers too." A ballad about him was sung in every country pub:

> John Wilkes he was for Middlesex,
> The greatest of the Shire,
> He made a fool of Mr. Bull,
> Called Parson Horne a liar.

The end came when he was seventy-two. Polly had just given him a drink. "Here's to my beloved daughter," he said, with the smile that had charmed many women. A few minutes later he died. He was buried in a vault in Grosvenor Chapel in North Audley Street. A memorial marble tablet has this inscription:

NEAR THIS PLACE ARE INTERRED THE REMAINS OF JOHN WILKES, A FRIEND OF LIBERTY.

The harlot's cry did not weave his winding sheet.

Plate 7 THE RAKE'S PROGRESS. The Earl surprises his wife and her lover and is mortally wounded. The rake escapes through the open window.

Plate 9 Sir Francis Dashwood ("Hell-Fire Francis")
at his devotions.

Plate 8 3rd Earl of Bute.
Prime Minister who visited
the Hell-Fire Club at
Medmenham.

11

POLITICS, PREACHING AND PROSTITUTION

Somebody once said that these callings should be left to
those who have a flair for them. The Medmenham monks
had an interest in all three vocations. Quite a few of them
were politicians, all had an interest in prostitutes, several of
them were preachers, the most prominent of these being the
Reverend Charles Churchill. He was as much fitted for such
a career as Dashwood and Sandwich were for their posts
as Cabinet ministers. Although he was a regular visitor to
the Abbey, Churchill had little regard for some of his
fellow monks. As a poet and a satirist, he used his pen to
flay them for their political intrigues. And although he had
little claim to virtue himself, he satirised their debauchery.
Sandwich and Dashwood put up some effort at maintaining
marital relations during their periods at home. As much a
failure as a husband as he was a parson, Churchill deserted
his wife after a few years of marriage. But let us deal with
Lord Sandwich first.

He married the daughter of an Irish peer, who was twice
his age. He was twenty-two at the time, an ungainly young
man and "as lecherous as a goat," according to the ever
watchful Horace Walpole, who also said that "Sandwich
could never get rid of the smell of brimstone."

In Drury Lane one day, a stranger to London asked a
friend who the tall man was shuffling along some distance
ahead. "That's Sandwich," was the answer. "He always
walks down both sides of the street at once." He was well
known as the most ungainly man in London. A fashionable
dancing master from whom he took lessons said, "I would
esteem it a great favour, my Lord, if you would never tell
anybody that you have been a pupil of mine." Both Sandwich and Dashwood were members of "The Dilettanti

Society," where the qualifications, according to Horace Walpole, were having been in Italy and the ability to hold great quantities of strong drink. At the gambling table, Sandwich would often play throughout the night and still arrive at his office in Whitehall about six in the morning. He expected his staff to be there punctually at their desks. No popping out to the nearest pub before the appointed hour of closing, as Charles Lamb used to do when he was a minor clerk in the India Office. When a senior official reprimanded him for coming to the office late, Charles said in his delightful stutter, "Yes, I know I'm late—but look how early I leave."

In spite of his ugliness, Sandwich seems to have had a way with women. He managed to seduce the wife of one of his friends—and he had very few—the Duchess of Bedford. Before Fanny Murray became his mistress, he had been accepted by Kitty Fisher, the most exclusive of Covent Garden ladies.

The delightful Kitty was so much in demand that she was able to set up a house of her own. Sandwich, who was her main customer at this time, came unexpectedly to visit her there one evening. It so happened that she was entertaining another of her admirers, Lord Mountford, a small man who looked like a drummer boy. A loud knock came at the door. Kitty hastily dressed and said, "This must be Sandwich." Whatever faults he may have had, Sandwich was a man of courage, who had fought more than a dozen duels, as a swordsman and a dead shot with a pistol. It was not the custom for gentlemen to challenge each other on a point of honour where a prostitute was concerned. But Mountford was not taking any chances and tried to escape through a window. Miss Fisher thought of a better plan. When Sandwich, having been admitted by a servant, was awkwardly climbing the stairs, Miss Fisher got Mountford hidden beneath her crinoline. She welcomed Sandwich at the door of her room, begged to be excused for a few moments and made an exit, Lord Mountford moving with her as if he had been the hind legs of a horse in a pantomime. Kitty Fisher must have counted the minutes till she could tell her friend, Fanny Murray, also a favourite with Sandwich, about this adventure. Miss Fisher was undoubtedly one of the brightest stars that shone around Covent Garden but Fanny Murray, thanks to John Wilkes, attained the greatest notoriety.

Fanny, of course, had many admirers, but she was seen round and about more often with Sandwich, so much so that Wilkes began his famous "Essay on Woman," with the line, "Arise My Fanny." When the character in *The Beggars' Opera* came front stage and said in an ominous aside, "That Jemmy Twicher should peach me, I own surprised me," the audience went into fits of laughter. Jemmy Twicher was Lord Sandwich and Jemmy Twicher he was to remain for the rest of his life. He was the object of ridicule in one cartoon and lampoon after another. *The Lives, Intrigues and Amours of the celebrated Jemmy Twicher* was a best seller. Fanny herself did not escape the attention of the pamphleteers who thrived on pornographic publications. All round the taverns and coffee houses, hawkers were calling and selling *The Amours of Fanny Murray and her Monkish Friends at Medmenham*. In the pubs where the gallants and their harlots met, they could buy "A Fanny Murray Pick-me-Up," "Fanny Murray's Nettle Juice" or "Gin and Fanny Sandwich." Would anybody doubt that the eighteenth-century Londoner who had something to sell made less use of topical publicity than his counterpart does today?

Sandwich, who had taken his seat in the House of Lords when he was twenty-one, became during the Fanny Murray period, the most unpopular man in England, not only with the masses but with some of his former friends in "The Order of St. Francis." Charles Churchill wrote of him :

> Too infamous to have a friend,
> Too bad for bad men to commend.

There was scarcely any crime in the calendar of which John Montagu, Earl of Sandwich, was not accused, from raping schoolgirls to sheer dishonesty as First Lord of the Admiralty, where his term of office was described "as unique in the history of the British Navy for incapacity." In his portrait by Knapton, possibly painted during the Divan

Club phase, he is shown in Turkish costume with a turban on his head, a flagon in one hand and a glass of wine in the other. The painter had caught something that helps us to understand the character of the man, the long sensitive face, the beautiful hands, the large eyes. One writer of the period praised him as "a patron of the arts, with a singular charm of manner," and went on to say that "few houses were more pleasant than his. It was always filled with beauty, rank and talent."

When that was written, Sandwich had discarded Kitty Fisher, Fanny Murray, even Santa Carlotta and taken into his home as mistress the only woman he had ever loved. Her name was Martha Rae, a fascinating girl who bore him four children. One became a British admiral, another a distinguished barrister and a third, a girl called after Augusta, Princess of Wales, married an admiral in the Italian navy.

The story of Martha Rae is one of the most tragic of the Georgian years. On the evening of April 7, 1779, she attended a performance of Dibden's *Love in a Village*, a pleasant operetta, at Covent Garden. Her mind was in turmoil as she enjoyed and hummed to the music. She was living in luxury with the ungainly and devoted Sandwich but in her heart she was in love with a young clergyman who was living on a pittance in a country parsonage. If it were not true, this story would have all the ingredients for a romantic novel. The curtain fell. Martha, attended by Lord Coleraine and other friends, came to the door of the theatre where her coach was waiting, with a coloured servant of Sandwich on his seat, ready to drive her home. As she came out of the foyer, a woman admired the red rose Miss Rae had in her bosom. No sooner had the remark been made than the flower fell to the ground. When she picked it up, the petals scattered and only the stock remained in her hand. "I hope this is not an evil omen," she said.

As she moved to the carriage, a man stepped forward and shot her through the head. Her body was carried to the Shakespeare Tavern nearby. The *Cornhill Magazine* had this report :

The crowd outside the theatre surged round the inn to look at Miss Rae's body, which Parson Hackman had just pistolled.

As the news of the murder spread round the West End and people rushed from the taverns and coffee houses to hear first-hand information, the coloured coachman whipped up his horses and drove away to bring the news to Sandwich. His master thought that he had come to tell him about some new trouble at the Admiralty, where a few days before an angry crowd had torn down the gates because the First Lord had ordered a popular admiral to be courtmartialled. When he heard what had happened, Sandwich pressed his hands to his head and said, "I could have borne anything but this." The student has to dig deeply to discover much of interest about the mistresses of the Georgian period, but there is much on record about the life and death of Martha Rae, in *Notes and Queries* and *The Dictionary of Biography*. Some say that she was "a milliner's assistant," which in those days was much the same as being a prostitute. There is, however, no evidence to show that she was ever one of the Covent Garden ladies.

The truth would seem to be that she was the daughter of a London staymaker and that she was apprenticed at thirteen to a draper in Clerkenwell. The most reliable reports say that Sandwich went into this shop one day to buy a neck-cloth and heard the girl humming in a beautiful soprano voice. He was so attracted by this and her girlish charm that he suggested she should have professional training. She was eighteen at the time and he was forty-two. The girl was flattered, agreed to the proposal and, as was bound to happen, became his mistress.

It was for her a glorious opportunity. She had always wanted to become a professional singer. Now she was taking lessons from the great Signor Giardini. She had her own coach to drive her when she wished to the opera in London. At the musical evenings which Sandwich held in his home, she was known as "the beautiful Miss Rae." As her children grew up she developed into a matron of great charm and beauty. Her reputation as a singer led to an offer to appear for a season at Covent Garden at a fee of £3,000. She refused, being perfectly happy to bring up her children in the old Tudor house in Huntingdonshire which was her home with Sandwich for fourteen years. She was the lady of the manor beloved by her servants and the villagers.

One evening by invitation to dinner came James Hackman, the son of a clergyman and a lieutenant in a regiment of foot. He fell in love with Martha at first sight. When she showed some interest in him, he wrote letters imploring her to leave Sandwich and become his wife. He decided to study for the church and was ordained, hoping that she would be more inclined to marry a clergyman than a soldier.

He wrote to her almost every day. She courteously refused all his offers, though she must often have longed to get away from the opprobrium of being the mistress of Sandwich and the jibes of the pamphleteers.

> When Lords turn musicians to gather a throng
> And keep pretty Misses to sing them a song.

The murder of Martha Rae was the only topic of conversation in London for weeks. One of the monks, George Selwyn, M.P. for Gloucester, who loved seeing blood spilled and attending executions, was out of town at the time. Many parsons in the Georgian era were a gruesome and libidinous lot. The Rev. Mr. Warner couldn't wait till he had rushed to his desk and write to his friend, Selwyn :

> I am obliged to confess some failure. I called coming from Coutts to the Shakespeare Tavern in order to see the corpse of Miss Rae and to send you an account of it, but I had no influence with the keepers and could not gain admittance.

There was more geninue compassion among the prostitutes for the death of Martha Rae than there was with the preachers or the rhymesters, who found only the tragedy another weapon to attack Sandwich :

> Our Navy Board seems hastening to decay,
> Since our First Lord has lost his brightest Ray

There was much more public sympathy for Hackman than there was for Sandwich. The young clergyman, thirty years her junior, was sincere and honest and madly in love. His one desire was to take her away from what he believed to be the evil influence of Sandwich. From her letters to Hackman, it is clear that she was more than fond of him. Soon after his ordination, he wrote to her passionately :

> I have ten thousand things to tell you. My situation here in Norfolk is lovely, exactly what you like. The parsonage house may be made very lovely at a trifling price. My happiness can be deferred no longer. Consent to marry me directly. The day I lead you to the altar will be the happiest of my existence. Oh, Martha, every day I live, I do but discover more and more how impossible it is for me to live without you.

He wrote to her again in March, a few weeks before he took the fatal decision :

> Though we meet tomorrow, I must write you tonight, just to say that I have all the hopes in the world. In a month or six months at furthest, I shall certainly call you mine. . . . By to-night's post, I shall write into Norfolk about the alterations to OUR parsonage.

Her attitude was that Sandwich had been kind to her and that she had the future of her children to consider. Her refusal to marry Hackman drove him to distraction. On the evening of the murder he dined with his sister, then went to his lodging in St. Martin's Lane and put two loaded pistols in his pockets. As she came through the door of the theatre, he edged his way through the crowd and fired the shot at close range. When she fell dead, he tried to shoot himself and lay on the street attempting frantically to beat out his brains with the butt end of a pistol.

At the trial at the Old Bailey, very little evidence was required. The story of what had happened was told by a few eye-witnesses, a woman fruit seller and a doctor. The jury without retiring could only bring in a verdict of guilty, though their sympathy lay clearly with Hackman.

One paper expressed the general feeling—"The murderer was forgotten in the lover." Boswell was so moved by the pitiful figure of Hackman in the dock that he not only was present at the trial but at a memorial service for the condemned man in Newgate Chapel. He told Dr. Johnson that he had hired a coach to follow the dray in which Hackman was carried to the place of execution near the present Marble Arch. Martha Rae was buried in the church-yard near her birthplace at Elstree, where there is a tablet to her memory. After her death, Sandwich went into retire-ment. Apart from his affection for Martha Rae and his love of music, there is little to admire in the life of Sand-wich. Charles Churchill meant every word of it when he wrote his epitaph :

> Wrought sin and greediness and sought for shame,
> With greater zeal than good men seek for fame.

Among the possible and known monks, three preachers have been named as members of the order—Edmund Duffield, Timothy Shaw, rector of Medmenham, and Charles Churchill, by far the most talented and intelligent of this clerical trio. As a poet, he takes a well-deserved place in English literature, as a preacher he has no claim whatever to distinction, as a libertine he was almost the equal to his lifelong friend, Wilkes, who had introduced him to the Abbey and to many courtesans.

Born somewhere in the neighbourhood of Westminster, the son of a poor parson, Churchill married a boyhood sweetheart, Martha Scott, and deserted her when he was a young curate, living on forty pounds a year. The marriage ceremony was arranged by one of the many touts around the city inviting couples to come to a prison and be joined in holy matrimony there by a parson serving his sentence for debt. Many young gallants persuaded girls to marry them in this way, had a brief honeymoon and disappeared. The fee could be anything from ten shillings to a pound. If the parson was so inclined, he would settle the deal for a bottle of gin. As many as five hundred marriages of this nature took place each month.

It is to the credit of Churchill that in spite of what he might have claimed to be an illegal marriage, he provided adequately for his wife when he became prosperous as a poet. By this time he had been unfrocked for intemperance and debauchery. He was the constant companion of the lively and lecherous girls like Effie in Tunbridge Wells, re-commended to him by Wilkes, who also introduced him to the orgies at Medmenham. But he was never quite happy there. Just as he preferred beer to wine, he had a greater liking for the more down-to-earth lasses to be found in the stewpots of the city than the society ladies or highly paid courtesans.

A great bulk of a man with broad shoulders and heavy jowls, he was caricatured by Hogarth as "The Bruiser." And a fighting parson he most certainly was. One of his colleagues said that if a row was brewing, Churchill would pull off his cassock and roll up his sleeves. We have only a few references to his visits to Medmenham. We hear of him singing bawdy songs with Wilkes in the golden ball tower above the church. We hear of him being offended because aged Paul Whitehead, Steward of the order, "a sedulous and patient seducer," had the choice of the younger nuns. According to Whitehead, Churchill was always stalking an elusive nun, Sister Agnes. "She," Churchill told a friend, "is the most fascinating of them all down at Medmenham." He was interested when Sister Agnes suddenly disappeared from the scene. In his book, *The Hell-Fire Club*, Donald McCormick tells how Churchill took one of the nuns on a summer evening for a stroll in the gardens and enquired what had happened to the girl he admired most. She told him that it wasn't very good manners to take her out only to talk about another woman. With real professional pride, she made it clear that she was there to amuse and please him. The only information he could get from her was that one of the nuns was pregnant and was being looked after by Sister Agnes. "Thank you," said Parson Churchill, "now you shall have your reward— in kisses and moonlit rapture. There is a better bed in nature's moss than in the monkish cells."

He was a great boy for the girls was Charles Churchill. The big affair in his life came when he met Elizabeth Carr, who was fifteen years old and the daughter of a London stonemason. This scandal sparked off a complete battery of literary squibs. It seemed that Betty Carr's parents had been urging her to marry an old and wealthy man. She preferred the now quite famous and silver-tongued poet, who was twice her age. A pamphlet printed anonymously appeared with the title, *A Modest Proposal about the Con-*

duct of a certain Reverend Gentleman in a Late Encounter.
It was as clever a piece of satire as Churchill ever wrote
himself.

> Let us imagine in our fancy, a young Lady in the Bloom of
> Youth, beautiful in her Person and endowed with many Per-
> sonal Accomplishments, whose unnatural father would force
> her to marry a person she had an utter aversion to. He is
> over Seventy Years of Age, deformed both in body and mind,
> diseased, avaricious and avowedly jealous. Who could blame
> her for making an escape? Where could she fly with greater
> Propriety for Protection than to a Clergyman? His function,
> his Character were safeguards for her virtue: and his being
> already married and a Father, were additional securities for
> her.

This delightful irony amused Churchill, even when Wilkes
wrote to tell him that the father and brother of Miss Carr
with a servant had gone to Kensington Gardens "with
pistols charged to assassinate you." Churchill replied :

> Assassinate—a pretty word fit for boys to use and men to
> laugh at. I never played yet for so high a stake.

The few years he spent with Betty Carr were the happiest
he had ever known. As in all his personal experiences, he
put his feelings into words :

> The mother trains the daughter she has bore,
> In her own parts, the father aids the plan.
> And when the innocent is ripe for man,
> Sells her to some old lecher for a wife,
> And makes her an adultress for life.

Everybody in London was talking about the parson poet
and his latest escapade. "A poet," wrote Horace Walpole,
"has forsaken his consort and his Muses and is gone off
with a stone-cutter's daughter." When the rumour spread
that the runaway lovers were in the Isle of Man, *Lloyd's
Evening Post* reported, that "The Late Reverend Mr.
Churchill, in order to take the benefit of privilege, is gone
to the Isle of Man. *The St. James's Chronicle* had a follow-
up :

> What's Churchill's business in the Isle of Man,
> An Essay upon Woman—that's his plan.

One of the admirable things of this period was the freedom of the journalist. If what they wrote about people like Churchill and Wilkes appeared in print today, the courts would be taxed to their utmost hearing libel actions. Next to Pope, the greatest satirist of his day in verse, Churchill, was as much in the news as Dylan Thomas or Brendan Behan were in this century. Few writers since have been better than the Georgian scribes at literary leg-pulling. The report on the Betty Carr elopement continued :

> Now whether the Young Lady was starved into compliance to marry an old Dotard, or whether she was in the Vigour of Youth, her warm blood running high (we will not say with Lust) enraptured with her Poet's Muse, his flowing Numbers, his Charming Diction, his Broad Shoulders, his Black Gown, his Amazing Parts, she had a mind to taste the delicious Fruits of Cytherea's Groves, it is a matter of no Great Consequence to an Englishman. After all it must be plain from this Excursion she is no backward lass and knows what's what as any girl in her Teens.

In his biography of Churchill, Wallace C. Brown has done most intensive research. He presents a portrait of a man who hated hypocrisy and pomp, cant and humbug. Hogarth's drawing of him as "The Bruiser" created the impression that he was a bully. The only evidence we have in this direction is his encounter with a publisher who had called him "a rude fellow." *The Evening Post* reported :

> We are informed that the encounter between a certain Genius and his Printer was as follows. The Genius took the Printer by the nose, who returned the compliment by striking his Antagonist a blow on the face, which so enraged the Herculean hero that he gave the Printer a blow between the eyes, the marks of which he will carry about with him for some time.

Of all the men connected with the orgies at Medmenham, Churchill was possibly the most likeable. He was certainly the most frank about admitting his own failings. When he contracted gonnorrhoea, he wrote to tell Wilkes about it with as little concern as if he had had the toothache. When he became wealthy, he started a home for prostitutes who had fallen on hard times.

Dashwood, who was a truthful man and not a malicious scandal-monger must be believed when he said that Churchill's home for poor prostitutes was "peopled with young girls he had seduced." With his imposing figure and his blue coat with metal buttons, he was one of the best-known characters around Drury Lane and Covent Garden. He was not ashamed to be seen in his clerical dress in a box in the theatre with one of his favourites, Lucy Cooper, a nymphomaniac whose insatiable desire for men was notorious. About a naked male statue in the garden at Medmenham, Churchill said, "The sight of it would make even Lucy Cooper run screaming from here to Covent Garden." His correspondence with Wilkes reveals much about his character.

> That I am a lazy dog need I say, that I am a drunken dog all men know, that I am an honest dog few but you will believe.

Few will deny that Charles Churchill was a fine English poet. As a libertine and drunkard, some may say that he was a disgrace to the Church. They might also apply this to the Earl Bishop of Derry, Dean Swift and many other brilliant men who were preachers. Churchill lived his short life fully. Soon after his elopement with Betty Carr, he was on his way to visit his friend, Wilkes, in France. He was thirty-two at the time. He died either in a fever or in a drunken coma at Boulogne.

12

HABITS OF THE MONKS

I am not a politician—but I have other bad habits.

Some of the monks at Medmenham had much worse habits than Artemus Ward could possibly have imagined when he made that statement at a political meeting in America. But their habits were no more corrupt than their politics. Let us consider the careers of some of the most important members of the Order of St. Francis, Dashwood himself, Paul Whitehead, a minor poet, and Bubb Doddington, "a vile man, ambitious, loose and never satisfied." "He wants to be a lord," wrote Walpole, "and when he is that he will want to be a duke."

The man who was born plain George Bubb achieved one of these ambitions when through his wealth and sycophancy he was ennobled and took the magnanimous title of Lord Melcombe-Regis. His mother came from an old Somerset family, the Doddingtons of Doddington. She married an Irish fortune-hunter, about whom we know very little. When her son, George, inherited the Doddington riches and estates, he added the maternal name to his own and become Bubb-Doddington. They were a strange lot, these Doddingtons. One of them shot a priest for no good reason except that he was a Catholic. Another with two friends consumed at one sitting two quarts of wine at the Bear Tavern in Leadenhall Street.

"They fell," the State Papers tell us, "immediately after this drinking bout into high fevers and deliriums, of which Mr. Doddington and another died." Another Doddington was appointed British Resident at Venice and got into a good racket of smuggling contraband between Italy and Africa. In this way, the family fortunes were amassed. Bubb's uncle was M.P. for Winchelsea, a seat which he handed over later to his nephew. Thus established with some influence, Bubb looked around for other means of making money. It was a time when England had acquired the right to supply some five thousand slaves annually from Africa to the Spanish colonies in South America. This was George Bubb's golden opportunity. He was twenty-two when he got an official trade appointment in Madrid. He discovered that the traffic was badly organised. When ships arrived at South American ports with a cargo of negroes, the markets were closed and the slaves had to be driven inland and sold at a loss. This clearly could not be allowed to continue. One of the first things Bubb-Dodding-ton did was to advise the South Sea Company "to send negroes often and in small quantities rather than in great numbers." If they didn't do this, he told them, they would have great quantities of the merchandise on their hands. "This," he said, "will prove a considerable loss to you as well as great hardship for the slaves." You will understand from this how considerate a man Bubb-Doddington was.

He worked it out that if 4,800 Negroes could be bought at from 250 to 300 dollars each and sold well, a profit of £300,000 at least could be made. There was no end to George Bubb's efforts to make the shareholders in the South Sea Company as rich as he was himself. Maybe this early interest in Negroes led him to take years later in London a beautiful coloured girl as his mistress and set her up in a house in Savile Row. In a fit of generosity, he signed a legal agreement with her and paid her £10,000 on the condition that he would not marry any other woman. She made a better deal than the thousands of coloured boys and girls Bubb-Doddington shipped to South America. There will be more about her later.

It would almost seem that Bubo or Sillybub, as he was known to many, had anticipated in his early life some such setting as the gardens at Medmenham for alfresco love making. Not lacking in scholarship, he translated while at Oxford, his biographer, Lloyd Saunders, tells us, some passages from Latin :

Sweet, sweet influence on lovers, thou who are present to soothe the breasts of maidens, thou who often bringeth back to me my elusive Corinna, come hither leaving the sunless caverns for a carpet of flowers.

You may be sure that he quoted these words to his friends, Lady Mary Wortley Montagu and Sir Francis Dashwood when the Hell-Fire Club was about to be promoted.

When he returned to England from Spain, Bubo got an appointment at £1,500 a year as Clerk of the Treasury of the Exchequer in Ireland, on the undertaking that he would not have to live in that country. He paid a deputy £50 a year for doing the job and kept the rest of the money. He became more affluent and influential when the unfortunate Frederick, Prince of Wales, made him court jester at Carlton House. This was an extraordinary establishment. The Prince had a bevy of young and pretty mistresses. Dashwood was a constant guest and made the most of his opportunities. Thomas Potter, another of the monks, son of the Archbishop of Canterbury and M.P. for the Cornish borough of St. Germain, was secretary to the Prince. The Bishop of Gloucester, William Warburton, who had married the lovely Gertrude Tucker, was the chaplain. Walpole refers to Gertrude as "a lively lady" and reported that Potter was "her gallant." Potter, in fact, was the father of her only child and was embracing her as assiduously as her husband was attending to the spiritual welfare of the Prince. Bubo was the major domo of the house.

Frederick was constantly amused by the great, fat ugly Teddy Bear of a man who flattered him at every possible moment. Bubo in a letter called God to witness that his one aim in life was to make the heir to the throne "a virtuous Prince." What better way than to introduce him to nuns at Medmenham.

If he was not a fully ordained member of the order, the Prince was a regular visitor to the orgies. He was the most likeable of all the Hanoverians, a man who spoke the language of the people. "I have just nicked Bubo for five thousand pounds," he told Potter, who agreed that anybody so rich as Lord Melcombe-Regis should be tapped as often as possible. A merry man who was never out of

debt, Frederick enjoyed himself by having Bubo now and
then wrapped in a blanket and rolled down a wide staircase
at Carlton House. We may be sure that Frederick's great-
grand-daughter, Queen Victoria, would not have been
amused. Bubo had no objection to being made a butt,
especially since it was also about to make him Lord Melcombe-Regis. He pulled every possible string to further the
interests of himself and his friends. Somebody described
him as "a fat, old rake, whose political somersaults were the
wonder of the age."

He was a fop who loved displaying his wealth. The bed
in his home at Hammersmith was embroidered with gold
and silver lace. His coat was adorned with the most expensive brocade. He drove through London in a grand coach
drawn by six horses. His uncle died before work had begun
on a great house he had commissioned Sir John Vanbrugh
to design for him at Blandford. Bubo had the job finished
at a cost of £140,000. When he had his home at Hammersmith redecorated he paid an Italian architect £140 a week
for supervising the work.

Money when he wanted to satisfy his vanity was no
object to Bubo. In spite of his generosity and lavish entertainment, he could never avoid being a figure of fun. On
receiving his appointment as a Lord of the Treasury from
George II, he knelt to kiss the royal fingers and could
scarcely get up again. The "comedian" king almost burst
his sides laughing. On another occasion, the queen was convulsed when the backside of Bubo's silken pants burst wide
open as he got up from his knees. Getting down on his
knees was one of Bubb-Doddington's more innocent habits.
Through his grapevine, Horace Walpole heard this story.
One evening, Bubo called at Savile Row to visit his
coloured mistress, Mrs. Strawbridge, about whom all we
know is that she was a very handsome woman. When he
entered her room, she was reclining gracefully on a couch.
He came forward, knelt down, kissed her fingers and said
passionately, "Oh, that I had you in a wood." Mrs. Strawbridge, a lady obviously with a sense of humour, didn't
bat an eyelid. "In a wood," she said. "What would you do
—rob me?"

Love-making in the physical sense was not Bubb-Dod-dington's strong point. At the best of times his boasted virility as a rake was merely a pretence. He saw himself as a bachelor gay, paying homage to one pretty woman after another. "I thank God," he told people, "that I am a single man."

The truth was that he had been married secretly for fourteen years to a widow, formerly a Mrs. Behan, who all the time kept discreetly in the background. Not even Mrs. Strawbridge, with her bond of £10,000, knew that her lover had a wife. It wouldn't have made much difference if she had known. Her house at Savile Row was little more than a retreat for Bubo when he wished to get away from the revels at Carlton House. He had a wonderful capacity for sleeping and could doze off at any hour of the day. He fell asleep when he went to the theatre, he fell asleep after dinner, he was asleep in the Abbey when one of the play-ful young nuns put the carrot and the turnips between his legs for the entertainment of her sisters and the other monks. The *Dictionary of National Biography* records that Lord Melcombe-Regis when he awoke would read verse and prose of "the coarsest nature, even when there were ladies present."

To look after his health, Bubo retained at fifty pounds a year a medical adviser, Dr. Thomas Thompson, who was also physician in chief to the nuns at Medmenham and the mixer of love potions for them and the monks. Here was one of the queerest characters of all the queer birds that nested at Medmenham. When in London, Dr. Thompson spent much of his time in the Cyder Cellar in Maiden Lane, where he talked incessantly about sex and disease in a voice which David Garrick said sounded "like a bumble bee on a window." He claimed also to be medical adviser to the Prince of Wales.

Bubo kept a room for his doctor at Hammersmith. It is on record that Dr. Thompson never cleaned his shoes and wore them till the toes could be seen. He wore his coat and trousers till they were threadbare. At breakfast one morning, Bubo ordered one of the servants to take away a muffin he didn't fancy. He looked at the decrepit ill-dressed Thompson and cried, "And take away this rag-a-muffin too."

This then was the domestic scene at Bubb-Doddington's home at Hammersmith—a wife who seldom appeared and a dissolute doctor, a retinue of servants and a host of hangers-on. No wonder Bubo spent most of his time in the gay atmosphere of Carlton House, with the monks at Medmenham or in Savile Row telling Mrs. Strawbridge what delights he would give her if only they could be alone in a wood.

Apart from the fact that he was one of the four most important members of the Medmenham fraternity, we know little about how he spent his days there. He was not a gambler nor a heavy drinker and he was well over sixty when the orgies were at their height. In his diaries, published after his death, he was careful to leave out any references to his pretensions as a rake. He was a close friend of Lady Mary Wortley Montagu, who was also in her sixties, though she is named as one of the nuns. It would seem likely that she and Bubo went to West Wycombe to see the younger people enjoying themselves. It may well be that the idea about founding the order began with Lady Mary, a daughter of the Duke of Kingston.

Her interest in clubs began when she was sixteen and the elite of the Kit-Kat nominated her as their standing toast of the year, an honour equivalent to being elected the Beauty Queen of London today. It meant that she would be eagerly chased by all the young bloods, which was, indeed the case. As a friend of Dashwood, though he was much younger, it is almost certain that she suggested the formation of a Hell-Fire Club and a monastery devoted to the worship of Venus. Lady Mary would have seen herself as the Mother Superior of the nuns, whether they came from the aristocracy, like herself and Lady Betty Germain, or from the bordellos of Santa Carlotta or Moll King. No better choice could have been made than Lady Mary as High Priestess of the revels. If she had been living in this age, she would have been the belle of bohemian Chelsea and a shining light among the London beatniks. Bubo, who liked stroking "little satin bottoms" and all the curves of the female form divine, would have been a devotee of strip-tease entertainment. A couplet by Charles Churchill, which has often been quoted, goes :

> Bubb is his name and bubbies doth he chase,
> This swollen bull-dog with lascivious face.

It is certain that no woman was ever in love with Bubb-Doddington. Lady Mary on the other hand had taken more adoring men in her arms before she was twenty than you could count on your two hands.

While still a girl, as Lady Mary Pierrepoint, she was in complete charge of her father's household, where the guests were mainly young men of rank and fashion, hell bent on seducing any young woman, whether she be a maidservant or the daughter of their host. "This early contact with the other sex," wrote one of Lady Mary's biographers naïvely, "could not be otherwise than destructive to maidenly modesty of manner which constitutes the charm of girl-hood."

The fact was that Lady Mary destroyed more men than had tried to conquer her. This Victorian biographer continued :

The incense lavishly burnt before the shrine of the noble young beauty by a multitude of titled fools and tuft-hunters developed her organ of vanity—originally large enough—to a prodigious extent.

Fair enough ! But there is another side to the picture of this Georgian lovely. As the daughter of a duke, she dressed like a queen on gala occasions. She was completely pro-miscuous and never permitted her heart to get involved in any romance. She was what we would call now "a good-time girl." If there had been purple hearts then, you may be sure that Lady Mary would have sampled them. When not on parade, she took little trouble about her toilet. In Paris, a young woman of the same social standing was candid enough to remark that the hands of her English friend looked none too clean. Lady Mary laughed. "Hands," she said. "If you could only see my feet." She had little good to say about the society ladies who sauntered through St.

James's Park or the men who went to look them over. She
wrote to a friend :

> In the first form of these creatures is a Mr. Vanberg. 'Tis
> certain he attends the Monday and Thursday market assem-
> blies constantly and for those who don't regard worldly
> advantage much, there's extra good and plentiful choice. I
> believe there were some two hundred pieces of women's flesh
> —fat and lean—last Monday.

When she was twenty-four and had done the rounds of
Carlton House with Dashwood and Bubo, Lady Mary
decided to select a husband for herself. Her choice fell on
a Mr. Wortley-Montagu, a pompous gentleman, who bom-
barded her with love poems as dull as he was himself. Lady
Mary may well have been of the same opinion as Samuel
Butler, when he wrote :

> She that with poetry is won,
> Is but a desk to write upon,
> And what men say of her they mean
> No more than on the desk they lean.

Mr. Wortley-Montagu was a desk-leaner and a high
grade civil servant. She left him in no doubt about her
feelings in the matter :

> Love is a mere madness—the passion of a child for a well-
> dressed toy. It delights a man till in a short time the tinsel
> covering wears through and he discovers that it is mainly
> made of sawdust.

The marriage was a complete failure. Mr. Wortley-
Montagu began to discover his mistake in taking a blue-
stocking as well as a wanton for his wife. After a month
or so of married life, she began to despise him. There was,
however, one advantage. She went with him when he was
appointed British Ambassador in Constantinople.

In Turkey, Lady Mary found much to admire. As she
watched the dusky Oriental women in the baths, she decided
that there was a lot to be said for nudity. "If," she wrote,
"the superfluities of dress are dispensed with, the faces of
women, in comparison with their figures, would attract
little attention." This was what she would tell her friend,

Bubo, when she got back home. He was of the same opinion
—that a naked woman was more an object of beauty than
a woman dressed. Lady Mary made a willing convert of
Sir Francis Dashwood and he agreed to the formation of a
club devoted to the worship of the female form. There is
no direct evidence about how the Divan Club came into
being at the Thatched Tavern in St. James's Street. We
do know, however, that both Lady Mary and Lord San-
wich were painted in Turkish dress. Dashwood had also
observed life in the East and had admired the facilities
given to men who could afford to keep a harem. In the
Divan Club, Sir Francis was already known as El Faquir
Dashwood Pasha. In the luncheon clubs a toast was always
drunk to "The Harem." It was a natural development for
men always in search of novelty to move from the confined
quarters of a room in a London tavern to a less restricted
retreat on the banks of the Thames. At "The Sign of the
George and Vulture" in Cornhill, The Hell-Fire Club was
duly constituted.

If the germ of the idea had come from Lady Mary, it
was Dashwood who thought of turning the abbey at West
Wycombe with its gardens in Buckinghamshire into a
thoroughly English setting where the rites of Venus could
be observed with both dignity and ceremony. Why should
solid English aristocrats have to follow slavishly the
example of the infidel Turks? There had already been
several Hell-Fire Clubs for the worship only of Satan. Why
not combine with this homage to the Goddess of Love?
The organisation, a major operation, was left to Paul
Whitehead. We know from the records that a seamstress was
asked to supply loose habits for twelve nuns. The monks
provided their own regalia. The gardens were laid out with
little alcoves here and there, with the great statue of Venus
and male figures like Grecian gods. The cells and the
Chapter Room were decorated with no expense spared. There
were plenty of boats on the Thames. Sir Francis had the
large gondola brought from Italy. The cellars were so well
stocked that liquor of every kind, worth £6,000, was still
there when the order was disbanded. Dashwood was
unanimously chosen as the head of the order. A strange

thing is that his name is not mentioned among the other founder members in that most reliable source of information, *The Dictionary of National Biography*. It is necessary to search elsewhere for the main facts about his life and his libertinism.

The man who was later Lord le Despencer came from a family of wealthy London merchants. His mother died when he was two years old and his father when he was sixteen. After a private education and a further schooling at Charterhouse, it was arranged when he was twenty-one —as was the custom for rich young men in those days—to travel on the Continent. Numerous stories are told about his behaviour on this tour. One Good Friday in Rome, he watched penitents gently beating their bare backs and shoulders with scourges and moaning in pretended agony. It was more than this young Englishman, already a confirmed atheist, could stand. With the impiety that continued throughout his life, he took a large whip from his great coat and gave the sinners a sound beating. It was not a prank to be admired, nor, indeed, were many of his similar vagaries in after life. Yet one of his most likeable qualities was the spirit of boyish exuberance which never deserted him. In London he went through the phase of beating up people in the streets, wrecking brothels and playing merry hell in the taverns. Women loved his gentle, whimsical face, his happy smile and his virility. When in Russia he was presented at court and became, according once more to Horace Walpole, the lover of the young and lovely Czarina Anne. He was never without a beautiful woman to amuse him. A lot that has been written about his sex life has been grossly exaggerated.

It is impossible to know what to make out of *Crazy Tales,* by John Hall Stevenson, called "Brother John of York" to distinguish him from Wilkes, "Brother John of Aylesbury," at the Abbey. "Brother John of York," who had a kind of Hell-Fire Club of his own in Yorkshire, wrote *"The Confessions of St. Francis and the Lady Mary, his Wife."* According to this story in verse, some of the London procuresses were Lesbians who used the younger nuns before handing them over to the monks. The *"Con-*

fessions" are supposed to be the story of one of these girls :

> I was taught at sixteen by a masculine nun,
> 'Til I learnt from a pistol to handle a gun,
> And then I encountered a Friar from Furnes,
> That used to serve her and the Abbot by turns.

> Now whether in Sappho 'twas passion or whim,
> She amused herself better with me than with him,
> So we struck up a bargain which pleased us all three
> I stuck to the Friar and she stuck to me.

> Between Friar and Knight, my Lesbian brother,
> I was like to become an unfortunate mother,
> But by her assistance and skill I miscarried,
> And at last by her means to Sir Francis was married.

Now there's a puzzling how d'ye do. In the first place Sir Francis did not marry a Lady Mary, though he had a half sister of that name, who may have been one of the nuns. The real Lady Dashwood was Sarah Ellis, a mystery woman if ever there was one. A good many years ago a few women novelists waged a bitter pen battle in the press. One of them scored a point when she wrote, "I am debarred from putting Miss Ethel Manning in her place, because she hasn't got one."

That statement could aptly be applied to Sarah Ellis. She does not seem to have any place at all in the Medmenham set up. The husbands of those days must be the envy of all married rakes today. No excuses about having to stay late in the office or being called off suddenly to Manchester on business. It was only a matter of mentioning casually, "I'm having a few nuns down from London for a week, dear," and the thing was fixed. Either Hall Stevenson invented his crazy tale about Sir Francis and Lady Mary or he didn't know about the existence of Lady Dashwood. We have proof that Sir Francis treated his wife with the utmost consideration. "One of the best women who ever lived," he told a friend when she died in 1769.

His experience of women had been wide and varied, from a maid-servant when he was little more than a boy to the young Czarina of Russia, Kitty Fisher, Lucy Cooper and Elizabeth Roach, who was one of his favourite Covent

Garden ladies for years. After his wife's death, he felt the need for a more permanent companion than could be found in the brothels. He had long fancied one of his tenants in London, Frances Barry, a buxom beauty who had begun her career at the Stock Exchange seraglio and was the mistress of a wealthy city man at Ludgate Hill. When Sir Francis made up his mind that he would like her, an arrangement was easily reached and the attractive Mrs. Barry took up residence at the Abbey, where she bore him a daughter. By this time, the Medmenham revels had come to an end.

Frances Barry was as faithful to Dashwood as he was to her until his death when he was seventy-three. He was a perfect example of a reformed rake making the best husband, though he and Mrs. Barry did not marry. A lonely man now, she was his greatest comfort. Most of all his friends, he missed Paul Whitehead, whose last wish was that his heart should be buried at West Wycombe. With his love of pageantry and as Colonel in Chief of the Bucks Militia, Dashwood saw that this desire should be carried out with military honours. The funeral procession he arranged is described in Chambers *Book of Days*.

> A grenadier officer in his uniform: Nine grenadiers, rank and file, two deep, the odd one last. Two German flute players: Two choristers in surplices, with notes pinned on their backs: Eleven singing men in surplices, two and two, the odd one last: Two French horn players: Two bassoon players: Six fifers, two and two. Four muffled drums two and two. The urn containing the Heart, resting on a bier ornamented with black crepe and borne by six soldiers, with three others on each side to relieve them: Lord Le Despencer as chief mourner, in his regimentals as Colonel of the Bucks Militia, with crepe round his arm. Nine officers in uniform. Two fifers, two drummers, Twenty soldiers with firelocks reversed.

The villagers of West Wycombe, who had often seen the great golden barge sailing down the Thames with the hilarious nuns and monks singing bawdy songs, watched this solemn parade in awe, with the resplendent Sir Francis as its central figure. It was so typical of him, this tribute to a man who had served the order well as its High Steward.

The son of a London tradesman, Whitehead was well past middle age when he became a monk. Apart from his office there, he seems to have spent most of his time at Medmenham writing pornographic verse about the nuns :

> Ye belles and ye flirts and ye pert little things,
> Who trip in this frolicsome round ...'
> Prithee, tell me from whence your indecency springs,
> The senses at once to confound.

Like Bubo, Paul liked stroking "little satin bottoms" with one hand and a glass of wine in the other :

> When Bacchus, jolly god, invites,
> To revel in his evening rites,
> In vain his altars, I surround,
> Though with Burgunaian incense crowned.
> No charm has wine without a lass,
> 'Tis she gives relish to the glass.

When Whitehead died, Dashwood had lost his most loyal friend. Potter and Churchill had died when they were young men. Sandwich and Wilkes were still alive but he had never been intimate with either of them. In some respects, he was the most honest man of the lot, especially in his political life. As Chancellor of the Exchequer, he admitted that he had no head for figures. He would have agreed with Wilkes when he said "Dashwood was put in charge of the nation's money because he was good at reckoning up tavern bills." Most of his biographers have dealt kindly with Dashwood. His London home at Pall Mall was an ever open house. Captain Edward Thompson, who wrote a life of Paul Whitehead, approved entirely of him and, indeed, of all the monks.

"They were," he wrote, "a set of worthy, jolly fellows, happy disciples of Venus and Bacchus, who got occasionally together to worship Women and Wine. To give more zest to their festive meetings, they enriched their own modern pleasures with the addition of classic luxury."

In this luxury, Dashwood spent his declining years, alone in his Abbey, with the faithful Frances Barry, who had probably made him happier than any other woman. It is difficult to assess his character, a considerate husband, a confirmed atheist who built churches, a generous contributor to charities, a rake and a most loyal friend. It would be difficult to improve on what Louis C. Jones wrote in his book, *The Clubs of the Georgian Rakes*. Let him have the last word about Sir Francis Dashwood :

> He was a man of laughter and wit, and of pranks. In the modern sense of the word he had no morals—there can be no question that he was a profligate—but chastity was a rare virtue among his peers, as every reader of Walpole, the magazines or newspapers of the time knows.

A great deal has been written about the masculine Georgian rakes. What about the most famous of the women who shared their pleasures?

13

COVENT GARDEN LADIES

Some men to business, some to pleasure take,
But every woman is at heart a rake.

Emma, Lady Hamilton, may never have been on the official
list of Covent Garden ladies issued by Jack Harris for the
information of the young rakes of London and visitors to
the city. Lady Hamilton, nevertheless, in her early days
knew what was going on in that district of the West End.
The daughter of a blacksmith in Cheshire, she had been
a children's nurse, a barmaid and a prostitute. She got her
first break when she became the chief attraction in "The
Temple of Health," which an athletic doctor, John
Graham, opened at Pall Mall in 1779. He announced one
day the appearance of "The Lovely Hebe Vestina, Rosy
Goddess of Health." This gorgeous creature, said Dr.
Graham, "will sit on her Celestial Throne and will exhibit
in her own person a Proof of the all Blessing Effects of
Virtue and Temperance and Recommend in these Effeminate Times methods by which Men may Regain their
Virility." The rosy goddess of health was the future Lady
Hamilton and few women of her time could have been
better suited for the part. A fresh country lass, she had a
perfect figure, with a bosom and hips to match. It was, I
suppose, no wonder that in spite of her vulgarity, she
captivated Nelson.

In his "Temple of Health," Dr. Graham, a fine figure
of a Scotsman, could be seen immersed in a mud bath up
to his chin. When he raised his muscular arms above his
head and displayed as much as possible of his magnificent torso, the ladies who had paid their shillings to come
in cooed in admiration. The men stood entranced watching
the beautiful Emma, also naked, her hair arranged in the

latest fashion, her face powdered, her neck and arms adorned with flowers and pearls. The light gauzy draperies of the celestial bed in which she reclined and moved up and down gracefully were perfumed with "the most costly essences of Arabia." The room was lit with soft lights and voluptuous music could be heard in the background. Other vestal virgins could be seen in a variety of poses behind thinly veiled curtains.

You paid a shilling to be admitted but the charge for the privilege of lying in the celestial bed would cost you a hundred pounds. It is a sad reflection on the times that not many were willing to pay this sum, although the temple was packed each evening at the bob a nob. That wasn't good enough and after a time Dr. Graham was obliged to close down. Emma was out of a job—but not for long. Her appearances in the celestial bed had brought her a host of admirers, who not unnaturally preferred to see her privately on a couch of their own selection.

One of the first of these gentlemen was Sir Harry Featherstonehaugh. Others followed, then Emma, as she put it in her own inimitable way, "got into giddy intimacy with the Hon. Charles Greville, nephew of Sir William Hamilton. She had a love nest with Greville for some years in a small house near Paddington Green. Through him she got to know George Romney, then one of the most distinguished painters. She sat for him in the nude, which was no great problem after her experience in "The Temple of Health." She also became his mistress. There is as Byron wrote, "A time in the affairs of women, which taken at its flood leads—God knows where." The tide was carrying Emma to a permanent place in English history. She was now a professional model. Romney passed her on to Sir Joshua Reynolds, who found her "the most bewitching" of all the women who had sat for him.

She owed a lot to Greville, who had engaged masters to teach her music and deportment. By no means a possessive lover, he was only too happy to make a gift of Emma to his uncle, Sir William Hamilton, who was greatly attracted to his nephew's mistress when he saw her for the first time. "She is better," he said, "than anything in nature." To cut a long and well-known story short, it is only necessary to say that before long Sir William and Emma were married. His job took him to Naples where Lady Hamilton was welcomed with open arms.

Her admirers were legion before Nelson came on the scene. When she was away from the city, the Earl Bishop of Derry, who was more often traipsing round the continent with beautiful women than he was in his Irish diocese, awaited her return with "the same solicitude as if he were a Jew looking for the coming of the Lord." When he was leaving Naples he wrote to her :

> Oh, Emma, who'd ever be wise, if madness were loving thee. Emma! I may not be able to look on your beautiful face for six months.

The Bishop, who was also the extremely rich Earl of Bristol, had a genius for finding new and lovely faces. Next to his pursuit of women, he liked building. As he watched workmen laying the foundations of one of the great houses he had erected in Ireland, a workman said as the boss was waddling slowly away, "A spade and a Bible would last his Lordship a long time."

If the Earl Bishop has his place among the great clerical libertines, Emma Hamilton, if not a fully qualified member, is in the select company of Covent Garden ladies. All were at heart the female rakes Pope wrote about in his *Moral Essays*. All through the ages, most women have had a special fondness for rakish men and few men have ever been madly in love with a prudish woman. The most beautiful of the Covent Garden ladies found men of both talent and wisdom. And, like Emma Hamilton, most of them were of humble origin.

The rank and file of Englishwomen have always been blessed with better looks than their sisters born in the stately homes. We have today preserved for us the fragile beauty of Nancy Parsons as Gainsborough saw her and the angelic face of Kitty Fisher as painted by Reynolds. Few women of royal or noble birth have had the grace and dignity of these two famous courtesans. It is not the custom now to make popular idols of our Nancy Parsons or our

Kitty Fishers. In their own period both of these lovely women were as much admired and publicised as the most glamorous film stars are today. Regally dressed and be-jewelled, they adorned the boxes of the most fashionable theatres. They were to be seen in all their glory at New-market and at military reviews. Sporting peers called their horses after Kitty Fisher. She was the toast in the most exclusive clubs. Secretary Pitt, the Great Commoner, whom Macaulay described as "the first Englishman of his time," was honoured to meet her when George II introduced them on a royal occasion in Hyde Park. Pitt bowed low and said, "I wish I had known you when I was younger."

Miss Fisher at the height of her fame was the most dis-cussed woman in London. She drove in the park in her open carriage drawn by six spanking, high-stepping grey horses in shining harness, driven by a coachman in bright scarlet livery.

Highly respectable Londoners would stop and say as she swept by, "Look, there's Kitty Fisher." Everything and everybody connected with her was news in *The Gentle-man's Magazine* or *Town and Country*, even her coach-man when he was accused of attempted rape on a girl of seventeen. Not even Kitty, with all her influence in high places, could save him, nor was the anger of the public of any avail when the death penalty was imposed. There were howls of disapproval when he was led to the scaffold and executed, with 150 soldiers present to restrain the furious mob who believed him innocent. "Farmer" George was now on the throne and was making a futile effort to suppress all forms of vice. The attitude of his Government to this death sentence was "that something had to be done to restrain the licentiousness of the times." It was in order for the Prime Minister and members of the Cabinet to have their fun and games with Miss Fisher but attempted rape by her coachman was a different matter. Kitty, at heart a deeply religious woman, brought up in a strict Lutheran family, had prayed that she might be able to have the verdict changed. Everybody knew that England then had the best judges that money could buy, but all her attempts at bribery failed. Her friend, Sandwich, could do nothing, neither could Lord Mountford or any of her other admirers. Although she had nothing to do with the fate of her coachman, she was for a time not quite so popular as she had formerly been.

Because of this, perhaps, she decided to walk abroad some days instead of being driven. As she strolled by Covent Garden one morning, a stranger, a dark young man, approached from behind and whispered with a foreign accent in her ear, "I love you." She had, of course, often heard these words before but in a different setting and not from such an experienced lover. Being already well supplied with men, she was not interested but was so amused that she chatted to the stranger for a time. He turned out to be the great Casanova, who had heard of her fame and felt the urge to see her. Nothing came of this brief encounter but in his *Memoirs* years later Casanova told how in London he had spoken to Miss Fisher, the most celebrated demi-monde then in the English capital. It was unthinkable for a rake from the country to visit London without at least having caught a glimpse of Kitty Fisher. He might as well have gone back home and told his friends that he hadn't seen St. Paul's Cathedral or observed the gay life in and around Covent Garden. Horace Bleackley in his book, *Ladies Fair and Frail,* quotes a letter written by a London rake to a friend in Derbyshire :

You must come to town to see Kitty Fisher, the most pretty extravagant little whore that ever flourished. You may have seen her but she is nothing till this winter.

This was the beautiful Kitty who had hidden the pocket-sized Lord Mountford under her skirt when Sandwich unexpectedly called.

Miss Fisher had a passion for horses. Many mornings she would ride side-saddle like a queen through Le Route des Rois, which the Londoner transmuted to the more understandable name of Rotten Row. Attended by two gallants she was galloping through Kensington Gardens on a highbred grey mare, given to her by one of her friends. When she came a cropper, the papers and the poetasters were provided with copy for a month. Ballads about the

occurrence could be heard in every tavern. One was called
"Kitty Fell" :

> Dear Kitty had thy only fall
> Been that thou met'st with in the Mall,
> Thou had'st deserved our pity:
> But long before that luckless day,
> With equal justice we might say,
> Alas! poor fallen Kitty.

The magazines read by top people reported the accident
as if it had happened to a member of the royal family. For
those who wanted pornography, one printer got out
hastily, *The Adventures of Miss Kitty Fisher,* a thoroughly
indecent publication which sold by the hundred at three
shillings a copy. But nothing written about Miss Fisher
could make her less desirable in the eyes of her admirers.
With her charm and wit, she would have been as successful as an actress as she was as a prostitute. She knew how
to dress to the best advantage and she had a figure that
was the envy of many women.

She could change her expression in a flash from a saucy
pout to a look of bashful innocence. Nobody could have
told that she had not been born in the lap of luxury or
educated by the best tutors. The truth was that her career
followed closely the pattern of so many other young women
with more than normal good looks and no money. She was
the daughter of a Soho tradesman of German extraction, a
preaching Lutheran who left her to fend for herself when
she was little more than a child. We hear of her living in
squalid lodgings in Paddington and nursing a consumptive
young man who died in her arms.

In all the records we have about the Georgian prostitutes,
the term "a milliner's apprentice" keeps cropping up again
and again. A girl thus described was almost sure to end
up as a harlot of one degree or another. Even in later years
when Charles Dickens wanted a setting where a pretty
young woman might be tempted, he chose to have Kate
Nickleby made an apprentice in the emporium of Madame
and Mr. Mantalini. You would have thought that the customers there would have been mainly society ladies. Yet
the innocent Miss Nickleby found herself being constantly

Plate 10 Tavern Scene (The Rake's Progress).

Plate 12
FANNY MURRAY. The Bath flower-girl seduced by Jack Spencer. Her 'protectors' included Beau Nash, Lord Sandwich, James Maclean 'the gentleman highwayman'. She ate Sir Richard Atkins' £20 note with bread and butter.

Plate 11
GEORGY'S DELIGHT. George IV and his mistress Lady Conyngham.

ogled at by Sir Mulberry Hawk and other would-be seducers. This was also the case with Miss Fisher. Unlike the virtuous sister of Nicholas Nickleby, young Miss Fisher, then a lively filly of sixteen, fell at the first fence.

Maybe there weren't any pretty barmaids then for idle young men to engage in flirtatious conversation, so it had to be a milliner's shop. Just as Lord Sandwich found Martha Rae in such a setting, so did "The Military Cupid," Tony Martin, a handsome young army officer, come across Kitty Fisher behind a counter. They arranged to meet, he showered gifts on her, made her presents of money and persuaded her to live with him in his lodgings. He soon tired of this arrangement and Kitty had to find some other means of making a living. She found her way to a procuress, Catherine Hayes, most likely, Moll King or Mrs. Goadby. For a girl of her youth and beauty, this was the only way to get on in the world. Her first protector was a Somerset squire. She went from him to a baronet, later to become the Earl of Lucan. He was so charmed with her freshness that he asked Sir Joshua Reynolds to paint her portrait. Reproductions of her as Cleopatra and as a girl sitting on a balcony were on sale in every fashionable print shop. Miss Fisher had arrived in a big way. She was to be seen with one or other of her admirers at the theatre and race meetings. For her now, it was only men of wealth and rank. Which of her noble lovers would propose marriage? That was the question many people were asking. The best bet was that it would be a horse-loving peer.

Lord Poulett was considered a possibility when she went with him to Newmarket to see race "Kitty Fisher," a mare he had called after her. Some thought that she would become the wife of Lord Pembroke, a keen racing man, who often went riding with her in Rotten Row. In the running stakes, Miss Fisher was the favourite. These were the days when the sons of the nobility often chose courtesans as their wives instead of the chorus girls whom their descendants made their ladies and their duchesses in Victoria's reign. Lord Sandwich and Lord Mountford were not considered likely candidates, nor was "Old Q," the Earl of March, who had too many women on his hands. In the end, Kitty made a good choice and became the lady Bountiful of a country manor.

It had taken her a long time to forget her first love. When "The Military Cupid" was in town, she would have broken any appointment to spend the days and nights with him. Now she had fallen sincerely in love for a second time, with John Norris, M.P. for Rye in Kent, and the grandson of Sir John Norris, Vice-Admiral of England, the hero of many naval battles and almost as famous as Nelson. After a runaway marriage in Scotland, which was declared illegal, the couple were wed again at a ceremony in St. George's, Hanover Square. There was strong parental disapproval of the union but the new Mrs. Norris soon broke down all opposition.

In those days a woman in her middle twenties was considered too old for a courtesan. They began usually about sixteen and were at their most desirable for the next ten years. Few of them were wanted when they reached thirty. It was a short life but a gay one. Kitty Fisher fully warranted the description as "the most pretty, extravagant little whore that ever flourished in London." She spent lavishly and generously all the money she had earned. One of her rivals, Fanny Murray, was offered five pounds by a lover and was so disdainful of so small a fee that she was said to have put the note between two pieces of bread and munched it. Kitty Fisher was known to have spent twelve thousand guineas in one year. When Edward, Duke of York, asked if he might call on her, he left fifty guineas on her dressing table when the session was over. Highly insulted by such a small gift from a prince, Miss Fisher gave orders to her servants that he was not to be admitted under any circumstances again to her house in Great Norfolk Street.

Now all this was over. No more merrymaking with the monks at Medmenham, no more dates to be kept with the Earl of March, "the old goat of Piccadilly," and so many more of the other roués she despised. Pope was only partly right when he considered that every woman is at heart a rake. At times the spirits of her Lutheran forbears appeared in her quiet moments and chastised her. She fought a continuous battle with her conscience—but she always won.

At her country home with honest, spendthrift, horse racing, gambling Jack Norris, she was the happiest of women. Each day on the beautiful mare he had given her as a wedding gift, she would ride at breakneck speed through the fields, clearing hedges with the best of the county horsemen. The villagers loved her, even when they had heard from the Cockney hop-pickers so many stories about her early life and notoriety in London. The sad thing is that she had such a brief period to enjoy the kind of life she had always desired. After a short illness which effected seriously her lungs, Kitty Fisher died at the age of twenty-nine.

No prostitute before or since in England was ever more beloved by the people than Kitty Fisher. It is doubtful if any woman in her profession will ever reach such eminence again, will ever have the finest racehorses called after her or have her portrait painted by the greatest artist of the day. On a Monday morning, April 9, 1759, when she went to his house in Newport Street for her first sitting to Joshua Reynolds—not yet a knight—Miss Fisher, "the milliner's apprentice," scarcely thought that she was to be immortalised.

14

HARRY, NAN AND FANNY

> When Harry ruled old England,
> And Fanny was a nun,
> When Nan went to the races,
> To see what horse had won.

The "Nan" of that verse from *The Gentleman's Magazine* was the lovely Nancy Parsons, the mistress of many noblemen and one of the most elegant models Gainsborough ever had. For him she was the ideal subject, with the sad, contemplative face of a nun, the long tapering fingers and the soft expressive eyes. Her portrait by Gainsborough is in private hands and would be worth a fortune if it were put on the market today. According to a pamphlet, *The Female Jockey*, Miss Parsons had her early training as a nun either with Santa Carlotta or an equally famous bordello run by "Mother" Welch in Cleveland Row. Even before she became one of the most powerful women in England as the mistress of the Prime Minister, she was able to earn a hundred pounds a day as a courtesan.

For established facts, it is wise for any historian to consult first *The Dictionary of National Biography* rather than depend on the gossip writers. This most reliable fountain of information tells us that Miss Parsons was the daughter of a Bond Street tailor. We have no knowledge as to whether he owned the shop or was a cutter of clothes for the Carnaby Street beaux of his day.

Like Kitty Fisher, Nancy loved the excitement of the racecourse. When her name came to be associated with the Prime Minister, Henry, Duke of Grafton, Horace Walpole wrote to tell a friend that "the affairs of the world have to be postponed because of a whore and a horse race." What a wonderful columnist Horace would have been if he were alive today and given a free hand in Fleet Street. But let us go back to Nancy before she met "Handsome" Harry Grafton.

In her father's tailoring shop, she met an adventurous chap called Haughton, an importer of merchandise to and from the West Indies. He took her off on a trip to Jamaica, on what you might call "a slow boat to China" honeymoon. What more could Mr. Haughton desire than a beautiful creature like Miss Parsons as a companion for such a tedious journey? She, however, didn't seem to care much for Mr. Haughton or Jamaica. She had a yearning for the bright candlelit taverns of Covent Garden and got the first available boat back to London.

All she brought home with her was the right to call herself Mrs. Haughton. When she became accepted as a Covent Garden lady, Horace Walpole said, "She is the Duke of Grafton's Mrs. Haughton, she is the Duke of Dorset's Mrs. Haughton, she is, in fact Everybody's Mrs. Haughton."

As Miss Fisher was known to the general public as "Kitty," Miss Parsons was soon spoken about everywhere as "Nan." Like Miss Fisher also, the name of Miss Parsons was appearing almost daily in the papers. As a change from his usual preoccupation with affairs of state, the editor of *Almon's Political Register* let down his back hair and published a long piece of satirical verse called "Harry and Nan."

> Can Apollo resist or a poet refuse
> When Harry and Nan solicit his Muse,
> A statesman who makes the whole nation his care
> And a nymph who is not quite as chaste as she's fair.

There was great tittle-tattle one evening at the King's Theatre, Haymarket, when Harry and Nan sat in a box together, with Queen Charlotte, you might say, as their next door neighbour. Harry's wife, the Duchess of Grafton, was sitting a few yards away in the dress circle. A racegoer on every possible occasion, Harry would always drive to a meeting with Nancy by his side. He was so fascinated by her beauty that he could go nowhere without her. If it had been applicable in those days, some bright journalist

would almost have put up the heading to an article—
"Harry get your Nan." Every now and then they would
spend a holiday quietly in France or in the English countryside. By this time, Nancy was getting a bit long in the tooth,
a fact that had not missed the Fleet Street boys. "Junius,"
the scourge of all politicians wrote :

> The Prime Minister of England, in rural retirement and in
> the arms of a faded beauty, has lost all memory of his Sover-
> eign, his country and himself.

The writers were now relentless in their attacks on
Grafton. "He had shocked all decent people by parading
his mistress in public." He had brought "his whore as if in
triumph" to the Opera in the presence of the Queen. Those
were typical of the comments appearing daily about Harry
and Nan.

As a journalist most of my life, I bow in admiration to
the gentlemen of the press in those bygone days. From the
dusty files of their newspapers and their magazines the per-
sonalities of many of them jump up like a Jack in the box.
They discreetly presented the news that Prime Minister
Harry Grafton had arranged for his marriage to his duchess
to be dissolved by Act of Parliament. Now—and how could
it have been better reported—one of them announced that
"The Duke of Grafton may part with his friend, Miss
Nancy Parsons, because he has found chaster connections."
You will note the delicacy of the choice of words. What
were these "chaster connections"? The tea cups tinkled
and the tankards clanked as people sought the answer to
that question. Although Miss Parsons could scarcely be
described as a "chaster connection," many thought that the
Duke would soon lead her to the altar. One journalist made
this prophecy, giving the lady a Christian name more suitable for what he considered would be her new station in
life.

> Anabella Parsons is now the happiest of women, attached to
> the most amiable man of the age, whose rank and influence
> raise her to power beyond many queens of the earth. Adored
> by the highest and adulated by all, her merit and shining
> abilities receive the applause that is justly due to them.

Could you beat that? Could any film star or courtesan of our day ask for better publicity? But, alas, it was not to be. Handsome Harry Grafton had found "a chaster connection" with Elizabeth Wrotesley, daughter of the Dean of Worcester. It was a sad blow for Nancy when she read about his wedding. She had been cruelly deserted but the wound was eased by the fact that Grafton had settled on her a life annuity of £900, not a princely endowment but enough in those days to get a girl by. The important thing was what to do next. Horse-racing men and gamblers seemed to be the right cue. She went to see "Old 'Q'," the Earl of March, who had been one of her early clients—but his harem was already full. She dallied for a while with the Duke of Dorset, a former lover. He, however, had taken a fancy to the beautiful daughter of a Methodist shoemaker, Betty Armistead, who had also been a nun with Santa Carlotta. Betty was a little over twenty, Nancy was now in her early forties. Her interest in the turf brought her a new lover, Lord Maynard, twenty-five years old and a complete dimwit. At the races one day, somebody asked him if he intended to take his seat in the House of Lords. "Good Lord," he said in amazement, "is that still going on?" Then he went off to see what Nancy wanted to back in the two-thirty.

On June 12, 1776, *The Morning Post*, then the paper which thrived on scandal, announced that Lord Maynard had married, "Mrs. Haughton, the late celebrated Nancy Parsons." The first thing the late Miss Parsons did was to trail her new husband off to Naples and take her place as Lady Maynard among the English colony there. This delightful city was then the capital of a kingdom where Queen Maria Carolina ruled with her dissolute husband, Ferdinand. Lady Hamilton had not yet arrived in Naples to become the confidante of the queen. Lady Maynard soon found favour with Maria Carolina and advised her on dress and other matters. She also found a new lover, Frederick, Duke of Bedford, who was eighteen and, like Dashwood and Sandwich, was making his first continental tour. By this time Nancy had grown tired of Maynard and they agreed to separate, especially since he had got himself

a new mistress, Mary Durville, who was soon to come to
London and join the elite of the Covent Garden ladies. It
is amazing how these girls got around.

We do not know how long Nancy held the Duke of Bedford, nor have we much knowledge of how she spent her
later years. Apart from contemporary references in the
eighteenth-century magazines and papers, there is very little
on record about her.

Horace Walpole called her "one of the commonest creatures in London, Everybody's Mrs. Haughton," which was
not true because Nancy was a choosy girl about lovers. That
she began as a prostitute in the cheap bordello of "Mother"
Welsh in Cleveland Row is most likely. Much more certain
is the fact that she was a woman of dignity, beauty and
intelligence. If she had become the wife of the Prime Minister of England, she would have held her own with any
lady in the land. She was eighty when she died in Paris
in 1814, a highly respected and charming old lady with
many memories of life in the reigns of all four Georgian
kings.

If the one hundred and sixteen years of Georgian rule
produced a magnificent crop of rakes, so did they give England its greatest courtesans, all women of humble birth who
broke down many social barriers. They acecpted the fact
that the princes, lords and statesmen they took as lovers
would exchange them as readily as schoolboys do with un-
wanted stamps in their collections. When Lord Derby had
no more use for Betty Armistead, he handed her over to
Lord Cholmondeley. Cholmondeley was glad to make a
present of another of his mistresses, Grace Eliot, to the
Prince of Wales, the future George IV, then twenty-one. He
denied at first that he was the father of the girl born to
Grace, who immediately had the baby baptised in St. Mary-
lebone Church as Georgina Augusta Frederick, daughter
of George, Prince of Wales. The Prince then graciously
acknowledged his parentage and made the girl and mother
financially secure for life.

Affairs of this kind were often settled generously, without any sordid court proceedings. When Fanny Murray had
the bailiffs in, she appealed to the son of Jack Spencer,

who had seduced her many years before in Bath and was
given an annuity for life of two hundred pounds. Not all
the Covent Garden ladies were as fortunate. Lucy Cooper,
the favourite of Dashwood and Charles Churchill over a
period of twelve years, died in obscurity. Betsy Careless,
"the gayest whore in London," finished up in a debtor's
prison. She had given the best of her youth to a rakish
young barrister, Robert Henley, who was to become Lord
Northington and Lord Chancellor of England. In the
theatres and taverns, these two were considered the most
handsome couple of all. When he was not escorting Miss
Careless, young Henley got rid of some of his youthful
exuberance by looting the common bawdy houses. It is to
his credit when as Lord Chancellor, he was reluctant to
have Wilkes indicted for publishing his *Essay on Woman*,
which made Fanny Murray in her respectable middle age
hide her head in shame. With his wealth and power, Sandwich cared little about the obscenity attached to his name
in the "Essay." Fanny had much more reason to fear the
publicity which followed when Sandwich read the filth
about her in the House of Lords.

If not the most successful, Fanny Murray had more freshness and charm than most of her contemporaries around
Covent Garden. Her first friend in London was Betsy Careless, daughter of a Smithfield tapster, and a woman now
in middle age.

When she saw the writing on the wall, Betsy Careless
opened a bordello of her own near Smithfield. But the competition from the established firms of Santa Carlotta, Moll
King and "Mother" Stanhoop was too great and Betsy was
forced out of business. Soon after she had taken Fanny
Murray under her wing, Betsy Careless disappeared into
the London limbo of the forgotten. That was the risk that
any prostitute had to take as she grew older. Fanny Murray
was more fortunate. As a flower seller in Bath, she attracted
the attention of the Hon. Jack Spencer, the grandson and
heir of the indomitable Sarah Jennings, Duchess of Marlborough, who was, you might say, the founder of the Churchill family. One of the Medmenham monks, Jack Spencer,
was by no means an admirable rake. He had seduced every

attractive young maidservant in the family home and was always on the look out for a new and lovely face. He found one in Fanny Murray. We have several descriptions of her when she was sixteen, "a fine gay girl, a blooming laughing dimpled beauty." It was the custom those days for the more lyrical lovers to write about the charms of their mistresses. Here is a prose portrait of young Miss Murray :

> At fourteen her person had already begun to testify marks of womanhood: her face a perfect oval, with eyes that conversed love, and every other feature in agreeable symmetry. Her dimpled cheek alone might have captivated, if a smile that gave it existence did not display such other charms. Her teeth regular, small and perfectly white, coral lips and chestnut hair soon attracted the eyes of everyone. Though inclined to be plump, she had delicacy enough in her shape to make it agreeable.

The Hon. Jack Spencer had little trouble persuading the lovely little flower seller to share his bed. She was completely enraptured by the experience and was hurt when he recommended her to his friends. There was no way out now. Fanny was the rage with the young rakes of Bath. As she walked along the street one day, a middle-aged gentleman was so attracted by her beauty that he asked her to call at his house. She remained there for three years, which were in one respect the most important in her life. Her elderly lover was Beau Nash, the acknowledged king of Bath, the arbiter of fashion in that city of elegance and beauty. He was kind-hearted, he taught Fanny how to dress to the best advantage and how to behave in polite society. It was a "My Fairy Lady" situation.

When she arrived in London young Miss Murray was an experienced and charming woman. She could use a fan with the best of the girls at the Cyder Cellar in Maiden Lane, the Turk's Head in Bow Street and the Rose Tavern in Russell Street. She soon became as well known in these rendezvous and as much in demand as she had been in Bath. "The Shakespeare's Head" was the place where the best clients could be found. When she had been a few years in London, Fanny's name appeared in the official *List of Covent Garden Ladies* as "a fine brown girl, rising nineteen next season, sound in wind and limb." She was, as Ned Ward would have said, passed "as physically, mentally and hydraulically perfect."

Fanny Murray was now the toast of London. Before Sandwich came on the scene, she had numerous lovers. It was thought for a time that she would marry the rich Sir Richard Atkins. When this rumour was current, Lord Chesterfield expressed the sentiments of some of the older peers when he wrote, "It is the fashion now for young fellows not only to deal with but to marry whores." It was considered the right thing to keep a common prostitute— but not marriage. Dammit all, a line had to be drawn somewhere or the country would go to hell!

One of Fanny's admirers was the son of an Irish clergyman, the highwayman, James McClean. This association came to a sudden end when he was hanged, sadly lamented by dozens of beautiful women. The time came when Fanny was beginning to feel the pinch. She was still attractive but she was twenty-seven. Beau Nash was dead, Sandwich was living with Martha Rae. Faced with imprisonment for debt, she appealed to the Churchill family and was graciously given a pension. The son of the Hon. Jack Spencer went even further. He arranged a marriage between Miss Murray and David Ross, an actor who had long admired her.

One of the most popular of London players at the time, Ross, a Scotsman, was a gambling spendthrift. In Fanny Murray, he got a faithful wife. He had no reproaches for her when the trial of Wilkes recalled her past.

Like most scandals, the amours of Fanny Murray were soon forgotten. "The fine brown girl, rising nineteen next season," had grown into an attractive matron. She was forty when she appeared as a dazzling "Queen of the Night" at a masked ball given in honour of the King and Queen of Denmark—the sister of George III—when they came to London. Mrs. David Ross was considered the most beautiful lady present. *The Gentlemen's Magazine* gave a glowing account of her dress and published her portrait.

A product of the hell-rakery of her time, Fanny Murray had only one choice about making a living after she had succumbed to Jack Spencer. She had been thrown "arsey-

varsey" into the business. In many ways she had been more
fortunate than many other girls who had willy-nilly become
prostitutes. In her youth, she had been the liveliest and the
happiest of the Covent Garden ladies, in spite of strong
competition. Among her rivals were several Irish colleens.
There was Nelly O'Brien, who had a fund of naughty
stories with which she could entertain any company of rakes
in her delightful Irish brogue. There was Kitty Kennedy,
the favourite mistress of one of her countrymen, Viscount
Palmerston. There was Polly Kennedy, the inamorata, it
was said, of one of the King's chaplains, the Rev. William
Dodd, who had founded a home for fallen women and came
often to visit Polly.

Nobody really believed that his friendship with her was
intended to lead her into the paths of virtue. There was a
twinkle in her smiling Irish eyes when she denied this
accusation of intimacy with the reverend gentleman and
said that she preferred noblemen as her lovers and didn't
approve of girls who stooped so low as to be the mistress
of a clergyman or an actor. Most of these Covent Garden
ladies were kindly law-abiding women who gave pleasure
to many men. Most of them would have like to end their
days like Fanny Murray, who died when she was forty-nine
in the arms of her husband at their home in Cecil Street
off the Strand. She had known most of the hard drinking,
gambling and duelling rakes of her time. Let us consider
some of them.

15

RIOTERS AND RAKES

A deed which shall with terror make,
The sons of midnight wrapped in flannel quake,
Frightening of cullies and bombasting whores,
Wringing off knockers and from posts and doors.

Those lines written in Queen Anne's reign might well apply
to hooliganism in our own century. They are one of the
first references we have to the gangs of young men, calling
themselves "The Hectors," "The Scowrers" or "The
Mohocks," who were the terror of London. One might as
well ask how or why they came into existence and enquire
why vandalism is rife today, why phone boxes are broken
open, why there are protection men, robberies and prison
escapes. There is not any simple explanation. It would
seem that every now and then through the centuries such
epidemics break out. "The Hectors" and "The Scowrers"
had their day. Their origin is obscure. There is, however, a
strange reason for the foundation of "The Mohocks."

In 1709, there arrived in London four Red Indian chiefs
of the Mohawk tribe. They had no intention of scalping
palefaces or doing a war dance at Charing Cross. As far
as we know not one of them carried a knife or a tomahawk.
They had come to England for the purpose of discussing
with the British Government ways and means of being
allowed to live in peace with the white conquerers of the
New World. Hollywood has proved that their mission was
unsuccessful. Possibly they found London less civilised than
the Wild West.

Anyhow, a few Covent Garden bucks when they saw the
Mohawks thought it would be a good idea to play at cow-
boys. They formed themselves into a Mohock club and went
rampaging as playboys of the West End world through

the streets by day and night. They chased harlots, beat up watchmen and used knives to slit the faces of honest citizens. Some people blamed the Government :

> You sent your Mohocks next abroad,
> With razors armed and knives:
> Who on night-walkers make inroad,
> And scared our maids and wives.

The sole purpose of the Mohocks seemed to be the wilful destruction of property and inflicting bodily harm on innocent people. They would enter a tavern with drawn swords and clear the house as quickly as any gunmen would in a Western epic. The servants hid behind the counters, the whores fled for their lives. The "Mohock's" were different from "The Roaring Boys" and "The Bravadoes" in the reign of Queen Elizabeth. They were concerned mainly with pranks such as the companions Falstaff had in the alehouses which Shakespeare knew. Some of them were professional thieves and pickpockets in a small way. They were not in the same class as James McClean, the gentleman highwayman, who was the darling of the ladies and who went in for robbery in a big way. He had always half a dozen lovely girls at his beck and call and expected them, like his prototype described by Ned Ward, "to calve at least once a year."

Around his swashbuckling handsome figure, a score of legends had arisen. He was the son of a lord who had taken to the road. He was a Robin Hood who robbed the rich to help the poor. He was a romantic lover whom any lady of quality would be proud to call her own. He was in fact, the son of a poor parson in the North of Ireland. Apart from being a devil among the women in Ireland, he led a quiet enough life there for a time as an apprentice to a linen merchant. Then the wanderlust came on him. After his father's death he got his hands on some money and went to England and set himself up as a wealthy squire. Gay and lively, always dressed in the height of fashion, he was to be seen constantly in the gaming rooms and in the company of the beaux and belles of Bath and Tunbridge Wells. He took a London house in St. James's Square, not far from the home of the prince of gambling men, Charles James Fox, son of Lord Holland. While McClean gambled in fivers, Fox would put thousands on the turn of a card.

Fox, however, though constantly in debt, could always depend on his father for money. McClean was forced to live on his own resources. His one idea for a time was to find a lady of fortune to marry him. But that didn't happen. He set up in business then as a matrimonial agent, promising his clients that he would provide them with wives worth at least £40,000. He meant well, did James McClean, but his luck was out both in the marriage market and the gambling tables.

The time came when he found it impossible to maintain his harem and live in style. When the money at last ran down, there was nothing else for it but to take to the road. All he needed was a brace of pistols and a mask. His first hold-up was at Hounslow Heath where he got sixty pounds from a drunken farmer reeling his way home. While the Mohocks were creating hell in the city centre, McClean would leave the gaming houses and take up his post at a quiet corner where he would be sure to find some midnight straggler with money in his pocket. One moonlit night, Horace Walpole was making his way from Holland House through Hyde Park when he was stopped at pistol point and relieved of his purse and some jewellery. He made such a noise about the value of his trinkets that McClean wrote him a polite letter offering him to exchange anything he had taken of sentimental value for its value in money.

By this time, the gentleman highwayman had become as famous as the Mohocks. Everybody was talking about the polite masked man who robbed wayfarers in such a genteel way. It was almost an honour to say that you had been one of his victims. The big coup came when James held up the Salisbury Flying Coach and did a real Dick Turpin act, treating the ladies with the utmost courtesy and requesting the gentlemen to stand and deliver. The trouble was that one of the gentlemen delivered a watch that he recognised later in the fob of James McClean.

The mystery was solved at last. The gentleman highwayman at Hounslow Heath and Hyde Park was the Irish squire of the gaming tables, the racecourses and the escort of many fair ladies. He was found and arrested in his lodgings "with twenty purses and a kept mistress." The trial of James McClean for highway robbery was a far greater sensation than any of the Mohock riots. Over three thousand people went to see him at Newgate. His gambling friends from White's Club were there to a man. Walpole recorded that "Some of the brightest eyes in London were in tears for McClean." Prints of his handsome face with the title "The London Hero" were on sale everywhere. He was the pin-up boy for all the romantic girls. After the trial, a minor author, Soames Jenyns, got out hastily a play, *A Modern Fine Lady*, in which one of the characters says, "She weeps because a handsome thief is to be hung."

Half of London and thousands of visitors from the country flocked to see the execution at Marble Arch on October 3, 1750. "Great ladies shed tears in abundance." An enterprising publisher brought out what he described as the startling revelations in *McClean's Cabinet Book Open,* which gave a list of "Duchesses, Countesses, Ladies of Virtue, and Misses," all of whom had, it seemed, been on the books of the gentleman highwayman.

Unlike McClean, the Mohocks were not interested in taking money by force but in hellery for its own sake. They were "gentlemen's sons who had lost their way," from the stately homes of England, from the parsonages and the Inns of Court. On one occasion young Lord Hinchinbroke and Sir Mark Cole were arrested and charged with having taken part in an attack on "The Watch." Although they had been armed with staves, they maintained that they were not Mohocks but had intervened to assist the guardians of the law. It was such a story as a boy told during an Irish riot when the mob dug up paving stones from the cobbled streets to hurl at the Royal Irish Constabulary. When asked why he had a paving stone in his hand, he said he had picked it up in case somebody might throw it at a policeman. Like Lord Hinchingbroke and Sir Mark Cole he was praised for a public-spirited act.

Many writers have given us accounts of the street gangs of London, especially Ned Ward and the poet laureate,

Thomas Shadwell, whom another poet, Nahum Tate, an Irishman who wrote "While Shepherds Watch Their Flocks by Night," described as "a mass of foul corrupted matter." In his play, *The Scowrers*, Shadwell seems to have been in sympathy with the tearaways of his time. He was certainly one of the boys himself, a hard drinking man, who loved the tavern life. In *The Scowrers*, one of the characters says :

> Oh had you seen him scowre, as I did, oh so delicately, so like a Gentleman! How he cleared the Rose Tavern. He and two other fine gentlemen came roaring in the handsomeliest, and the most genteely turn'd us all out of the room, and swinged us, and kicked us about, I vow to God, it would have done your heart good to see it.

Every night a bunch of the boys would whoop it up in the Rose Tavern or some other saloon where the harlots were sitting quietly minding their own business. When they had created havoc indoors, the Mohocks took to the streets around Clare Market.

> I beat twenty Higling women, spread their butter about the Kennel, broke all their eggs, let their sucking pigs loose, scowred like lightning and kick'd fellows like thunder, Ha, Ha. I wiped out all the milk scores at the Doors. I went about serenading with six Fiddlers in a Dung Cart. Ha, Ha, what a frolic!

What a frolic indeed! No respectable woman would dare walk out alone at night. Even the prostitutes were driven from their beats, in case they would be trussed up and rolled down Ludgate Hill. Dean Swift was one of the few men who ventured out at dark. He wrote to tell his beloved Stella about the gangs in London "cutting people's faces every night, but they won't cut mine." Ned Ward who knew more about the haunts of vice in London than any of his fellow journalists has an amusing story about another clergyman, as little afraid as Swift was of the marauders. A mild little parson, he asked permission when attacked if he might be allowed to preach a sermon. A repentant "scowrer" told Ward what happened :

> He said we'd given him too short a warning for a good

sermon—but he'd do his best. He told us we were wanderers
on the earth—like the Apostles. And like the Apostles, he said
we were looked down on by the rich—and so, he said, I suppose are you. The Apostles, he said, were driven into gaols
and put in pillory. Their calling, he said, often brought them
an untimely death. And so, he said, if you'll forgive me mentioning this, an untimely death may well be your fate. But
there is one difference, he said, between you and the Apostles.
They ascended to Heaven—and he pointed to the sky—and
your destination, he said, if you'll forgive me mentioning it, is
maybe in the opposite direction.

If Ned Ward and Shadwell were inclined to treat the
"Scowrers" and the Mohocks as a joke, Queen Anne and
her advisers took a more serious view. In March, 1712, a
royal edict went out offering a reward of a hundred pounds
to any person who would give information "about the
number of Evil-Disposed Men who were creating Great
and Unusual Riots and Barbarities in the open streets." But
still the atrocities went on. Men had their face slashed,
women were stripped and indecently assaulted, windows
were broken, shops looted and carriages overturned.

Every coffee house and tavern had their "chuckers-out."
Every brothel had its bully armed with a cudgel to make
sure that the girls and their clients could go about their
business in peace. The gangs of professionals as distinct
from the gentlemen rakes would accept protection money.
Most of the hell-raisers, however, came from the upper
classes, as may be seen in a drawing after the style of
Hogarth in the British Museum.

It shows a crowded scene at Covent Garden where rakes
are playing havoc with citizens and their womenfolk. One
young man is embracing a lady who looks too frightened
to protest. A man is sprawling on the ground as the beaux
in cocked hats and knee breeches are laying about him
with staves. A girl is being pursued, two boys look on in
fear and amazement. The scene is described in verse :

> They sally forth and scour the street
> And play the devil with all they meet,
> Swagger and swear and riots make,
> And Windows, Lamps and Lanthorns break.

The Women struggle, scream and scratch,
Loud swear the men—in come the Watch.
See one who tho' he risk his life
Will from a husband force his wife,
As rudely his companions treat
All that in petticoats they meet.

If, as occasionally happened, some of the young rakes
were arrested and brought to trial, the penalty would be a
fine of two or three shillings. If you had influence in those
roistering days the law was lenient. The infamous Lord
Mohun was brought before the House of Lords on a charge
of being party to a murder. Fourteen of his peers found him
guilty and sixty-nine brought in a verdict that he was innocent. In the minds of all honest people there was no doubt
whatever about his guilt. After a drunken session, Mohun
and a friend had stabbed to death an actor, William
Mountford.

They had followed him from the theatre to a house in
Howard Street off the Strand and brutally attacked him.
The only motive seems to have been that he had been paying too much attention to the lovely Mrs. Bracegirdle, who
was his leading lady. Mohun was one who believed that
actresses should not take a lover unless he was a lord. To
the noble Mohocks, a player and a parson belonged to the
lower stratum of society. When they were not chasing
women, the sons of the wealthy used up their surplus
energy in politics and gambling. One who spent much time
in all these pursuits was Charles James Fox, the second
son of Lord Holland of Holland Park. Papa Holland en-
couraged young Charles James to be a man about town,
even to the extent of supplying him with plenty of money
to lose in the gambling dens.

Young Fox won £7,000 one evening at cards and lost it
on horses next day at Newmarket. His father bought him
a seat in Parliament for a constituency in Surrey. He also
paid his debts which came in one year alone to £140,000.
With his red-heeled shoes, his scarlet cloak and his hair
with a blue rinse, Charles James Fox was a rake, a fop and
a libertine, with a silver tongue which he used to advantage
in Parliament and as a lover. He set up house with Betty

Armistead, an enchanting Covent Garden lady, in Chertsey, where the Prince Regent used to visit them and pour out his heart about his deep love for Mrs. Fitzherbert.

Always ready for any kind of wager, Charles James Fox, like so many other men with lashings of money to spend, got involved in one of the great gambling events of his day—the decision whether or not the Chevalier D'Eon was a man or a woman. You would have thought that this was a matter that could have easily been determined. But that was not so. None of the interested parties seem to have taken the simple way out of debagging the Chevalier and settling the question of his sex beyond any shadow of doubt. The only reasonable explanation of the mystery is to be found in a pamphlet some years after D'Eon's death.

The theory put forward in this account is that the Chevalier, who had been living on gambling in London for five or six years, was short of money. Some method of raising the wind had to be found. A doctor called Hayes made an arrangement with a moneylender to put up the sum of £700, on which interest would be paid until such time as a verdict on the sex of the Chevalier could be reached. The news spread round the gaming clubs. Bets were laid to the extent of sixty thousand pounds. The popular question was "Tell me gentle hobble-de-hoy, are you girl or art thou boy?"

When the moneylender brought a legal action for the recovery of his money, two doctors hired and paid for the purpose examined the Chevalier and decided, with his agreement, that he was a woman.

The news of this momentous decision spread like wildfire. "D'Eon is a woman. We knew it all the time." John Wilkes went post-haste to Medmenham to tell the monks at the abbey that the Chevalier should have been counted among the nuns. The doctors had decreed that the Chevalier behaved like a woman, that he wore women's clothes, and that several men had testified to their personal knowledge of his femininity. Some were still of the opinion that the Chevalier was a man. They cited the case of Harriet Snell, who had passed most of her life as a man and was then, at the time of the D'Eon judgement, married and

living as a woman. When D'Eon died in 1810, a post-
mortem showed that he was a man. What function he
performed as one of the monks at Medmenham is something we shall never know.

These then were the golden years of the Mohocks, the
gamblers and the fighting men. In vain did Queen Anne try
to improve the morals of her people. In vain was it laid
down that no brothel owner "should keep any woman to
board except at her own pleasure." In vain did the law
say that no woman should be kept "in a bawdy house on
Holy Days."

Each year some fifty years ago there came to London an
Irish rake who spent his money and applied to Bernard
Shaw, an old school friend in Dublin, for a loan. G.B.S.
once sent him this letter :

My dear ———. I am in receipt of your hardy annual.
You ask for five pounds. I enclose ten. With this you may be
able to get drunk today, tomorrow and perhaps the day after.
But for the love and honour of God—and Holy Ireland—
keep your fare back to Dublin.

Let us begin now to consider how holy Ireland compared
with England in the great days of Georgian rakery.

16

IN HOLY IRELAND

Dublin is a city of poets and philosophers—all loitering with intent to work.

Whoever made that remark—and it was neither Shaw nor Wilde—might well have added that the capital of my native country has also been noted through the centuries for its gambling and its fighting men. The greatest of them all was "Fighting Fitzgerald," nephew of the Earl Bishop of Derry, himself enough of a rake to approve of this son of his sister, the Lady Mary Hervey of Bristol. On his paternal side, George Robert Fitzgerald came from a family of landed Irish gentry. The wild blood of his Celtic ancestry mixed with the eccentricity of the Herveys produced a character unique in the story of Anglo-Irish rakery. As a boy he went to Eton and later to Trinity College, Dubin, where his chances of taking a degree of any kind were so remote that his parents thought it advisable to buy him a commission in the Dragoon Guards, then stationed in the West of Ireland. In his uniform, he was a commanding and handsome figure.

He felt certain that no woman could resist him. Swaggering past a tobacconist's shop in Galway Town, he saw a pretty dark-eyed colleen behind the counter. He went inside, flashed her a smile and asked for snuff. As her back was turned, he grabbed her in his arms and tried to rape her.

When she screamed for help and half the men of Galway ran to her assistance, "Fighting" Fitzgerald drew his sword and fought his way back to the regimental headquarters. This was the first of many similar episodes. His reputation spread round the countryside. The dragoons were disliked by the Irish peasantry. Fitzgerald was feared, even by the county squires. It was a case of "lock up your daughters" when he went visiting. With the assistance of his Uncle Fred, the bishop, he found and married a woman with a fortune of £10,000. With as much as he could get of this money and his private income of a thousand a year, he went to Paris. He remained there for two years, gambling, fighting, drinking and maintaining several women. When he had exhausted all the gay life that France had to offer, he came to London.

One of the first things he did there was to apply for membership of the exclusive gambling club run by Mr. Brookes, who had the difficult task of telling him that he had been blackballed. He insisted that there must have been a mistake. Nobody could do such a thing to an Irish gentleman and a Hervey from Bristol as well. The select committee of the club, with a retired admiral as president and a number of lords as prominent members, was in session. Pushing his way past Mr. Brookes, Fitzgerald ran up the stairs burst into the room and demanded to know who had been guilty of putting in a black ball against him. The company was silent. Fitzgerald drew his sword.

He went round the room demanding of each man present, "Was it you?" One or two said, "No," a few were silent, nobody answered yes. "I knew that Mr. Brookes had made a mistake," said Fitzgerald. "Since nobody has put in a black ball against me, I must be now a member." The scene that followed was described afterwards in anecdotes by Richard Brinsley Sheridan about club life in general. The members of Brookes ignored Fitzgerald. They formed themselves into small groups and went on talking as if he wasn't there. "Old Q," the Earl of March, could be heard muttering something about balls of lead in the backside of the intruder was what he deserved more than black beans in a ballot box. Fitzgerald called the waiter and ordered champagne all round so that his fellow members might drink his health. The waiter hesitated. "Go and tell Mr. Brookes to send up the drink," said Fitzgerald, "and tell him to make no more mistakes about black balls." When the bottles arrived, the members were silent. Fitzgerald did the only thing possible under the circumstances—he lowered the lot himself. According to Sheridan, he bade the members good-night and never returned again to Brookes. They were an odd lot, some of these members. One of them used to come in with a bridle and a halter in his hand leading an imaginary racehorse. It was no place for a man like "Fighting" Fitzgerald.

No other old Etonian, as far as I know, has ever excelled Fitzgerald in hellery. One day at Vauxhall Gardens, the Rev. Henry Bate, owner and editor of the *Morning Post*, was walking with an actress, Mrs. Hartley, who was, as it was put so nicely in those days, "under his protection." Fitzgerald, who didn't care much for parsons, thought a lovely actress should have found better company. He passed some lewd remarks about the lady and her escort. You would have thought that Mr. Bate would have shown some Christian forbearance and let the matter drop. He was however, a fighting parson. He made it his business to see that the incident which followed got full publicity. "Mrs. Hartley," he reported, "was so completely put out of countenance by the impudent stare of Fitzgerald that she burst into tears." Mr. Bate demanded that honour should be satisfied. Fitzgerald agreed that this should be done, not with swords or pistols but with bare fists. His modest proposal was that he and Mr. Bate should strip naked and fight the matter out like men. "Mr. Bate," says the report, "was thunderstruck."

> Although he was by no means afraid of the issue, he did not choose to fight in a way unbecoming to a gentleman. He considered the proposal vulgar and could not agree to such a display unbecoming to a man wearing his cloth.

That seemed fair enough but something had to be done. Friends of both gentlemen tried to bring about an amicable settlement. Mr. Bate was an old Harrovian, Fitzgerald was Eton.

As one public schoolboy to another, the parties agreed to forget the incident and apologies were exchanged all round. "This curious affair," wrote a contemporary of Fitzgerald, "made a great noise at the time." The gentlemen shook hands, spent some time in pleasant conversation and were perfectly reconciled. The only injured person was Mrs. Hartley, who must have felt hurt that Mr. Bate cared so little about her that he was not even prepared to defend her honour in the nude.

Fitzgerald had inherited something from his Uncle Fred, who was equally fond of pranks. For the entertainment of some of his lady friends on a sandy beach near his bishop's palace in Ireland, he insisted that a few of his curates and some nonconformist clergymen should compete in a horse race bareback. But all the frolics of Uncle Fred were like Sunday school outings in comparison with the escapades of his nephew in later years.

When his wife was dead and his fortune vanished, he returned to Ireland and set up a Fitzgerald gang, which he led in a series of attacks on people and property. He was arrested and sentenced to three years imprisonment. He made a daring escape and turned his country mansion into a fortress, from which he and his men opened fire on a regiment of horse artillery sent to dislodge them. When at last the siege was coming to an end, the gang took to the hills, killing any man who stood in their way. For food they robbed farms and shot game.

After a number of fierce skirmishes, "Fighting" Fitzgerald and his men were cornered and marched off to the prison at Castlebar. At his trial, he made such an eloquent speech that the judge was all but reduced to tears as he pronounced the death sentence. The scene at the execution, as described by an eye-witness, reads like highly coloured fiction.

Four clergymen, two Roman Catholic and two Protestant, attended Fitzgerald on the way to the scaffold which had been erected in the square of the town. Regiments of dragoons stood by in their scarlet uniforms as the parsons prayed. When the rope was placed round Fitzgerald's neck and the lever pulled, he fell to the ground and at once got up. The rope had broken and he was still very much alive. "Be Jases, sir," he said to the sheriff, "you ought to be ashamed of yourself. That rope wasn't strong enough to hang a dog let alone a Christian. Go and get a stronger one and don't be long. I haven't much time to waste." A new rope was brought and the old Etonian, George Robert Fitzgerald, was hanged, at the age of thirty.

In his early days, he had been a member of the Dublin Hell-Fire Club, which resembled "The Order of St. Francis of Medmenham" in all respects, apart from the absence of nuns to enliven the proceedings. The Dublin gentry preferred to find their mistresses among the strapping daughters of their tenants.

These Anglo-Irish hell-rakes were quick on the draw. It was not the custom of some of them to ring a bell when he wanted a man servant to bring him more drink or a maid to come and amuse him. He merely picked up a loaded pistol and let fire at some target in the room, a chandelier, a mirror or a piece of furniture. This was undoubtedly an expensive way of dealing with a domestic matter but it had the advantage of bringing the man or girl hastily to obey the summons. It was usually one shot for a man servant, and two shots for the current mistress among the maids. The more bullet marks there were on the walls or the ceiling the more the master had to show his friends.

A prominent member of the Dublin Hell-Fire Club was Colonel John St. Leger, a racing, gambling rake who had done the London rounds of the stewpots with the Earl of March and the Prince of Wales. He and the prince had been lovers of Grace Eliot and had for a time shared Betty Armistead and other Covent Garden ladies.

In *Notes & Queries*, there is a story about St. Leger and the Duke of Rutland, then Lord Lieutenant of Ireland. St. Leger, a regular visitor at the Vice-Regal lodge, was so enamoured of Rutland's far from chaste wife that he sat in admiration one day as, after eating some greasy morsels with her fingers, she washed her hands in a basin. As an act of gallantry he arose, filled a glass of water from the basin and drank the lady's good health. She was charmed with the compliment.

So indeed was her husband. A roué of long experience, he sat observing the incident with composure. "You're in luck, St. Leger," he said. "The Duchess will, I think, be washing her feet before dinner. I'll instruct a servant to place a goblet of the water on the table for you."

St. Leger was famous in Ireland for his celebration of the Black Mass, which put the fear of God into the hearts of the peasants on his estate. Some of their descendants will tell you that his coach and his horses still travel round the country at night driven by a headless coachman. Legends about the Regency buck of Ireland will live for ever. A friend of St. Leger and a member of the Dublin Hell-Fire Club, was "Jerusalem" Whaley, so called because of a trip he made to the Holy Land. His father was known as "Burn-Chapel" Whaley, a staunch Protestant who felt it his duty to burn every Roman Catholic church around his large estates. When he died, his son, Tom, inherited all the property and a large annual income. When he was sixteen, he set off for Paris with a most suitable tutor, whose first job there was to set up a private harem for the sole use of himself and his young master. When they grew tired of this diversion, they went to the gaming houses where young Mr. Whaley got involved with a few card sharpers and lost £14,000 in one evening. The harem had to be closed.

They managed to keep two pretty Parisian prostitutes and brought them back to Ireland. When he was nineteen, Tom Whaley got himself elected M.P. for a seat in Co. Down. He spent more time gambling than he did in Parliament. He bet a few friends one evening a thousand pounds that he would jump from a window in Stephen's Green in the heart of Dublin, land in the first open carriage going by carrying an attractive woman and kiss her. He won without any difficulty. His most successful wager was made when he said that he was growing tired of life in Dublin. "Where will you go," he was asked. "To the Holy Land," he said. "Is anybody willing to bet £30,000 that I won't get there, play handball against the walls of Jerusalem and be back in Ireland in two years' time?" The offer was accepted, so off young Whaley went and returned with documentary evidence to collect his winnings.

The problem now was what to do next. He had contended with bandits and pirates on his round trip between Dublin and Jerusalem. Was there any place left where he could find a new adventure. He had heard that a revolution was about to take place in France. Why not go there? So off he went to Paris, where he arrived in time to witness the execution of Louis XVI, a man after his own heart. The city wasn't what it used to be. All the brothels were closed. Gone were the lively girls he had known as a boy of sixteen when he was there with his tutor. The gentry were being guillotined every day. Raging Madame Defarges were crying in the streets for more aristocratic heads to fall. No clubs where you have a bet. No racecourses nor theatres. Not a prostitute anywhere in sight. Even Jerusalem was better than this.

He decided that he had seen enough of Paris. For some time he had been considering writing his memoirs. Where would he begin the job? He had never cared much for London. He had lost interest in Ireland's green and now far from pleasant land, where a revolution was pending. The Dublin Hell-Fire Club had fizzled out like a damp squib. The only thing was to go home to the arms of his mistress, Ann Courtney, to whom he was greatly attached.

He had begun to consider that it was time to settle down with her and their two children. And where do you think he decided to go? To the Isle of Man. He returned to England and had plans prepared for a house that would be their home. He arranged to have shiploads of clay for the foundations brought from Ulster so that he might end his days on Irish soil. When Ann Courtney died, he was a comparatively poor man. He wrote in his "Memoirs" :

> I was born with strong passions, a lively imagination and a spirit that could brook no restraint. I possessed a restlessness and activity of mind that directed me to the most extravagant pursuits : and the ardour of my disposition never abated till satiety had weakened the power of my enjoyment, till my health was impaired and my fortune destroyed.

To Ireland during the Georgian years, the English brought much that was good. They built some of the finest examples of Georgian architecture in the British Isles. They made Dublin one of the foremost centres of the drama in Europe. They brought with them also a tradition of rakery. This began in earnest after the Battle of the Boyne and

William of Orange was king. Philip, Duke of Wharton, whose father had helped William in his Irish conquest, inherited large Irish estates. Before he was twenty-one, he took his seat in the Irish House of Lords, at a time when women were being raped in broad daylight in the Dublin streets. In such a way did the Anglo-Irish gentlemen pass the time.

The reputation of Wharton in England for blasphemy and debauchery had followed him to Dublin. In London, the pamphleteers had called him "The Doorkeeper of Hell." His women associates were known by such colourful names as "The Lady Fornication" and "The Lady Sodom and Gomorrah." As far as libertinism and eccentricity went, Dublin was almost on a par with London. When the Duke of Bedford was Lord Lieutenant, it was his whim to dress up as a countryman and steal out from the Vice-Regal lodge and go to see the fun and games at Donnybrook Fair. In a brawl there, he was hit over the head with a porter bottle. A handsome young man who was standing nearby recognised the Duke and thought that it was "a very provocative thing" to treat the King's representative in Ireland in such a way. A claret bottle possibly, but nothing so common as a porter bottle! The young man, John Loftus, got the Duke away from the fracas and decided he might use the occasion to his own advantage. Next day, elegantly dressed, he presented himself at Dublin Castle and gave a servant a note marked "Private and Confidential." The Duke with his head bandaged received the visitor and thought it would be wise to close his mouth and have the Donnybrook affair kept secret. He made young Loftus an official at his court, where there was a plentiful supply of handsome maids. He cast his eye on Mary Brennan, who was not only a beauty but the possessor of a good voice.

They set out together on a tour of Ireland. John Loftus himself described their adventure:

> I gave out in every town that we were playing at wandering minstrels for a large wager. Our success was great. People believed me to be a lord and Mary a lady. I played, she played, and we both sang very well. Nobody offered us less than silver and sometimes gave us gold.

In such a delightful way did the Anglo-Irish gentry pass their time. When he returned to Dublin, the boss at the Vice-Regal Lodge had an interesting job for Loftus. The French, as had been long anticipated, had landed in Ireland, at the seaport at Carrickfergus in Co. Antrim. The Duke thought it would be a good idea if Loftus should travel up there and find out what was going on. What had taken place was a most polite and gentlemanly invasion.

François Thurot, son of a French father and an Irish mother, and the commander of a privateer, had come ashore with a few hundred men. After a slight opposition, his good manners charmed the mayor of the town and all the inhabitants. The girls were delighted with the French sailors. There was a sing-song each night and plenty of lovemaking. All was going well until a British flotilla was sighted with Loftus aboard. Thurot decided that it was time to leave the Irish shore and sail away. Sad farewells were said as they rowed back to their ship. There was widespread grief when the British flotilla engaged the privateer off the coast of the Isle of Man and Thurot was killed in the action.

All through the days of the Georgian kings, there was a considerable two-way traffic between England and Ireland. The English sent over their dukes and their lords to govern the country and an odd bishop, like the Earl of Bristol, to look after in his own way the spiritual needs of the Protestants. The Irish exported actors and actresses by the dozen and writers—Congreve, Farquhar, Goldsmith, Swift and Sheridan, who had his early education at Harrow. Like "Fighting" Fitzgerald, despite their public school background, Sheridan was blackballed at Brookes' Club. He gained admittance in a much more subtle way than Fitzgerald. He knew the names of the two members who had voted against him at the ballot, which usually took place in the early hours of the morning. He had messages sent to both, to tell one that his London home was on fire and to inform the other that his mistress was being attacked by another lover.

When the two gentlemen went hurriedly off to deal with these problems, Sheridan's friends put up his name again and he was unanimously elected. Before long he was the most popular and a leading gambling and drinking man in the club. His wit and charm endeared him to the Prince of Wales, who liked him in preference to all his other friends for a trip round the bawdy houses at night. Dressed as country yokels in smocks, off the Prince and Sheridan would go from Brookes to the lowest brothel of all, "The Salutation," run in Tavistock Court by an Irish woman, "Mother" Butler.

Sheridan was one of the best customers on the books of Mr. Brookes. He seldom laid a bet for less than a hundred pounds. When he popped in on his way to or from the theatre, his drink was a half pint of brandy to be knocked back neat. He was a chip off the old block, Tom Sheridan, a man of the theatre of whom Dr. Johnson did not approve. "What has Sheridan done for the drama?" he asked in one of his more petulant moments. "He might as well burn a farthing candle at Dover to show a light at Calais." If Tom Sheridan did little for British drama, his son set ablaze some lights that have been burning in the theatre for two hundred years. As proprietor of Drury Lane, Richard Brinsley Sheridan was never out of debt. Somebody once complimented him by saying that his productions always went like clockwork. "Quite right," he replied. "It's all—tick—tick."

Nobody, indeed, was ever better at getting tick than Sheridan. He had like so many Irishmen a deeply rooted objection to paying the bills of tailors and wine merchants. When proceedings were taken against him for a long overdue account, including some money lent, the wine merchant concerned instructed his lawyer not to go on with the case. "Has he paid you?" the lawyer asked. "No," said the wine merchant. "He's ordered some more wine for a party and borrowed another ten pounds." Well might he have said himself as in the epilogue to *The School for Scandal*:

> Save money! When I've just learnt how to waste it!
> Leave London! When I've just begun to taste it.

Holy Ireland has produced few greater sons or more loveable rakes than Richard Brinsley Sheridan. The friend of kings and princes, the lover of beautiful women, the hard drinker and gambler, the wit and the spendthrift who was always in debt to money-lenders. He was having a good laugh at himself when he made one of his characters say, "When he is sick they say prayers for his recovery in all the London synagogues."

So ends this story of rakes and robbers, gangsters, gamblers and the rest. "All the times are now reformed," said Dryden. What do you think?